# Roots of the
# Western Tradition

# ROOTS OF THE WESTERN TRADITION:
## A Short History of the Ancient World
## Third Edition

**C. WARREN HOLLISTER**
University of California, Santa Barbara

**JOHN WILEY AND SONS**
New York   Santa Barbara   London   Sydney   Toronto

*Library of Congress Cataloging in Publication Data:*

Hollister, C. Warren
    Roots of the Western tradition. A Short History of the Ancient World.

    Bibliography: p.
    Includes index.

1. History, Ancient.        I. Title.
D59.H64    1977                     930                 76-51394
                                                        76-51530

ISBN 0-471-40720-8

Printed in the United States of America

10 9 8 7 6 5 4 3 2 1

# Preface

This book is the first of a series of five paperback volumes covering the span of Western Civilization. The other volumes in the series are *Medieval Europe: A Short History* by C. Warren Hollister, *The Renaissance and Reformation* by John F. H. New, *Prologue to Modernity: Early Modern Europe* by James D. Hardy, and *A Short History of Europe since Napoleon* by Roger Williams. The first two volumes in the series are available in condensed form as a single paperback, *Odysseus to Columbus*. And the entire series, with some condensation and editorial changes, is published as a one-volume paperback, *River through Time: The Course of Western Civilization*.

The third edition of *Roots* has undergone a page-by-page, word-by-word revision for the purpose of achieving greater clarity and accuracy and incorporating the results of recent research. Changes have been made at many points—the treatment of the Isis-Osiris myth, the Hebrew prophets and the Babylonian Captivity, the role of the Dorians, the circumstances of the battle of Marathon, early Greek monarchy, the Athenian Empire, the Greek response to Alexander the

Great, the role of Cicero in the Roman Senate, the reforms of Augustus, the literature of Rome's Silver Age, and the constitutional changes wrought by Diocletian and Constantine. More fundamentally, the political evolution and class divisions of the Roman Republic have been reinterpreted, and recent, more sympathetic treatments of the Late Roman Empire have been incorporated into the text.

In this edition, as in previous ones, it has been my goal to strike a proper balance between factual narrative and interpretation, to maintain the highest possible level of accuracy, to present sound, current interpretations, and to write clearly and, if possible, vividly. Above all, I have sought brevity, in the belief that the beginning college student needs a genial and agile guide through Western Civilization rather than an encyclopedic, overillustrated catalogue of facts. With the conviction that the great textbook has yet to be written, I have tried at least to write a succinct one that will leave adequate time for the student to pursue extensive collateral reading. Annotated guides to such reading, both in modern works and in the sources, are provided at the ends of the three parts into which this book is divided.

A number of scholars have been extremely helpful in making suggestions for this revision and previous ones. I am grateful to Alfred J. Andrea of the University of Vermont, to Frank J. Frost, Harold A. Drake, and Judy Thorne, all of the University of California, Santa Barbara, to Mortimer Chambers of University of California, Los Angeles, to William G. Sinnigen of Hunter College, and to many other reviewers for their helpful critiques. My thanks also go to Sally M. Vaughn and Thomas K. Keefe for reading the galley and page proofs of this third edition.

C. Warren Hollister

# Contents

# List of Maps

*Maps by Russell H. Lenz*

# List of Illustrations

# Roots of the
# Western Tradition

# PART ONE

# THE ANCIENT NEAR EAST

# 1

## The Birth of Civilizations

There are those who believe that history is obsolete. The present is said to be so radically different from the past that we have nothing to learn from former generations or previous ages. This view, which finds its most ardent supporters among those most ignorant of the past, cuts us off from the flow of history and prevents our seeing human society in its proper perspective: as a river through time. The ideas, experiments, blunders, and labors of many generations underlie the modern technological marvels that have revolutionized our standard of living and our means of polluting and killing. Our political and economic institutions—parliamentary, capitalist, communist, socialist, fascist—are products of long historical processes. The same is true of our ways of thinking about religion and social justice and urban planning and astrophysics, our achievements in medicine with their byproduct of overpopulation, our sense of what is moral and what is obscene. These are not matters unique to us but aspects of our own moment in the evolution of an age-old civilization. Only the most indifferent can fail to wonder about the roots of the

culture that surrounds us, shapes our assumptions, defines
our options, and governs the very categories in which we
judge and perceive.

The Western cultural tradition stretches back some 1200
years into the European past. It rose from the debris of a still
older civilization—the Greco-Roman—from which is derived
much of its political, artistic and philosophical orientation.
Western Civilization draws also from the Judeo-Christian tradition of the Ancient Near East, which was inspired in turn
by the more ancient religious thought of Mesopotamia, Egypt
and the lands between. Greco-Roman civilization was itself a
child of former cultures: Minoan, Etruscan, and, behind
them, Egyptian and Mesopotamian. This connected sequence
of civilizations extends, like an immense chain, backward
some six thousand years to Mesopotamia's emergence from
the Stone Age and forward into an unknown future.

What do we mean by civilization? Various simple defini-
tions have been suggested at one time or another, but none is
entirely satisfactory. Civilization is usually associated with
the town or city (the Latin *civitas*), yet the people of ancient
Egypt were more or less evenly spread through the Nile valley. The population of the valley was dense, but there were
few cities. Do we associate civilization with writing? This art
was unknown among some of the ancient civilizations of the
Americas.

Civilization can only be regarded as a configuration of several elements, all of which are products of a fairly high degree
of social organization. It is best understood not in the abstract but in the concrete, as a convenient label for a whole
series of related developments such as were occurring in the
Nile and Tigris-Euphrates valleys between about 4000 and
3000 B.C. As the fourth millennium opened, the Near East
was a mosaic of Neolithic farming communities,* nomadic

---

*The Neolithic Age, or "New Stone Age," was itself the product of a revolution-
ary change in the Near East, thousands of years earlier, from the traditional hunting economy to a new economy of farmers and herdsmen.

herdsmen, and peoples whose livelihood still depended on hunting and fishing. By 3000 B.C. in Mesopotamia the village was giving way to the city-state, a political unit that was much larger and more complex than the Neolithic community. This momentous process was accompanied by a series of fundamental discoveries and inventions: writing; mathematics; the widespread use of copper and, shortly afterward, bronze; monumental architecture; a calendar; large-scale irrigation systems; and administrative bureaucracies. Collectively, these developments mark the transformation from primitive society to civilization.

These same processes were occurring in the Nile basin. Although the city was less prominent in Egypt than in Mesopotamia, the Egyptians were centuries ahead of the Mesopotamians in achieving political unity. By 3000 B.C. the entire Nile valley had been organized into a single state. The fourth millennium, which witnessed the birth of civilization in Mesopotamia and Egypt, was in some respects the most creative era in human history.

How does it happen that a civilization is born? The historian Arnold Toynbee, in his *Study of History*, explains this mystery as a process of challenge and response. The Nile and Tigris-Euphrates valleys presented a challenge: they could be exploited only by an elaborate system of irrigation and flood control. The Egyptians and Mesopotamians made the appropriate response and thereby created civilizations. The barren and mountainous lands of Greece presented another challenge to which the Greeks responded by taking to the sea and dominating the commerce of the eastern Mediterranean. But Toynbee's hypothesis, although suggestive, fails to explain adequately why the same kinds of challenges sometimes evoke responses and sometimes do not. Most scholars have therefore preferred to stress the unique elements in the rise of each specific civilization.

Most civilizations, however, have one common element. Despite the individuality of their own styles, ideals, and viewpoints, almost all have been strongly stimulated, especially in

their formative centuries, by older civilizations. There is even
reason to believe that the Egyptians themselves, their intense
originality notwithstanding, were influenced by the slightly
earlier Mesopotamian example. The Mesopotamians also seem
to have provided certain stimuli to the earliest civilizations of
the Indus River in India and the Yellow River in China. To
this rule of external stimulation there are only two clear exceptions: the civilizations of the New World, which origi-
nated much later; and Mesopotamia itself. The civilization
that emerged during the fourth millennium in Mesopotamia
was not only the first in man's history but also the only one
in the Eastern Hemisphere to rise completely by its own
bootstraps.

# 2

---

# Mesopotamia

**Civilization Arises in Mesopotamia: 4000 to 2800 B.C.** | Mesopotamia lies in the valley formed by two neighboring rivers, the Tigris and Euphrates. The name is derived from the Greek words *mesos* (middle) and *potamoi* (rivers) and means, literally, "between the rivers." The birth of civilization in this region can best be understood not by seeking some elusive master key to historical process but by looking at the geography, environment, and culture of Mesopotamia itself during the fourth millennium.

For thousands of years the entire Near East had experienced steadily decreasing rainfall. Grasslands slowly became desert wastes; the valleys of the Nile and the Tigris-Euphrates, once densely overgrown swamps, gradually became habitable. As the accompanying map shows, the Tigris-Euphrates valley is actually a long strip of fertile lowlands with a highland region to the northeast and the Arabian desert to the southwest. The rich lowlands of the valley form the eastern part of a large semicircular region whose western extremity runs along the eastern Mediterranean coast. This "Fertile Crescent," arching northward from the Mediterranean and the Persian Gulf, was throughout history an alluring prize for both the northern hill peoples and the southern desert peoples.

Most of the earliest Neolithic villages were established in the highlands to the north, where people had migrated long before in search of rainfall. The valley itself presented special problems. Its soil, replenished annually by the rich silt of the flooding rivers, was vastly more fertile than the soil of the northern hills, but the swamps had to be drained, the water of the rivers had to be distributed over the dry land, and above all the destructive floods had to be mastered.

The valley presented its inhabitants with both a mission and a reward. Drainage systems would control the floods, thereby making settled life bearable, and would also bring water to the thirsty soil. Once these systems were built, the ever-renewed soil would produce crops in such abundance as the hill dwellers had never imagined. The Neolithic villages were simply inadequate to this task, but larger communities arose that were able to direct sizable quantities of labor toward a common goal and to irrigate relatively large areas. As a consequence of these efforts, the rich land produced a significant surplus, and the wealth was thereby created with which the new states could expand. No longer was everybody obliged to work the soil; other careers were now possible. The vast majority remained on the land, as they would until recent times, but a crucially-important minority began to specialize in such things as war, administration, craftsmanship, trade, and service to the gods.

Such was the process that produced civilization. The evolution can be understood in part as a series of historical causes and effects, but at the core of the matter there remains an element of mystery—of volition—perhaps even courage. One can analyze in retrospect the possibilities of the situation, but one cannot explain adequately why they were grasped and exploited by those specific people at that specific time.

**The Sumerians** | The people who built the earliest civilization

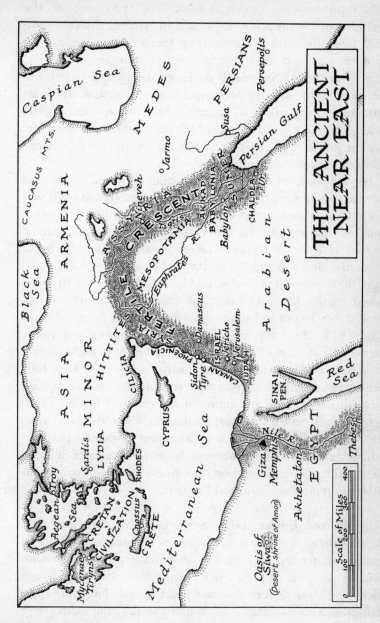

The Ancient Near East.

in Mesopotamia are known as Sumerians. Their language, the
first human tongue to be expressed in writing, differed radically from the dialects spoken by the Semitic peoples who
were to play a central role in later Mesopotamian history.
The culture of the Sumerians outlasted its creators to become
the nucleus of all later Mesopotamian civilization. Their architecture, their mode of writing, their literary and artistic
styles, and their attitude toward life and toward the gods per-
severed in the Valley of the Two Rivers and its dependent
territories throughout antiquity.

The outlook of the Sumerians and their successors was
profoundly pessimistic. Nobody can say exactly why this was
so, but the Mesopotamian environment doubtless had something to do with it. To the ancient Mesopotamian, nature
seemed violent and unpredictable. No matter how he tried,
he could never really tame the fitful and uneven floods.
Sometimes the water level would be inadequate, and drought
would result. At other times the raging waters might break
through the levees and submerge whole towns. Even as late as
A.D. 1831, the rampaging Tigris burst its dikes and swept
into Baghdad, annihilating 7000 homes in one night. Mesopotamia was a land of extreme contrasts. Long weeks of blis-
tering heat might be followed by torrential rains that turned
field into marshland and immobilized the population. There
were furious winds and suffocating dust storms. Moreover,
the fertile valley was open to incessant raids and periodic
conquests by envious tribesmen from the northern hills or
the southern desert. In short, the heavy price of civilization
in Mesopotamia was constant insecurity.

**Religion And Culture** | The Sumerians projected this ever-
present dread into their conceptions of man and his gods.
Early man tended to regard all inanimate objects as person-
alities with wills of their own. Mountains, trees, rivers, even
sticks and stones, were alive and had volition. The more spectacular aspects of nature—the wind, the sky, the earth—were
usually regarded as gods. Today people regard the world
around them as inanimate—as an "it"—but primitive peoples

thought of the world as animate—as a "thou." To them, humanity and nature were linked by an "I-thou" relationship.

The Sumerians, awed and terrorized by nature, saw themselves as its plaything. They were impotent before its invincible power, tragic figures subject to the whims of the gods. "Mere man—," the Sumerians observed, "his days are numbered; whatever he may do, he is but wind." The delights of heaven were not for mere humans; the scanty allusions to the afterlife in Mesopotamian literature represent it as a state of darkness and gloom.

Being an agricultural people, the Sumerians recognized the regularity of nature, the daily sweep of the sun, and the annual procession of the seasons that governed the rhythm of planting and harvesting. Accordingly, their chief deity was the sky god, Anu, and their most beloved was the earth goddess, Inanna, who symbolized fertility. The worship of the Earth Mother is a product of the Neolithic Revolution, when the invention of farming suddenly made the fertility of the soil all important; she is represented by a crude figurine discovered at the Neolithic village of Jarmo, and she retained her importance (under a variety of names) throughout antiquity. But the Sumerians had other deities far less benign than those of earth and sky. Enlil, the god of the storms, symbolized force and destruction, wildness, and violence. Against the orderly sequence of crops and seasons, Enlil represented the terrifying, unpredictable side of nature.

Helpless before nature's wrath, the Sumerians saw themselves as slaves to the gods. This theme of human bondage appears vividly in the Mesopotamian Epic of Creation, where it is said of man, "Let him be burdened with the gods' toil, that the gods may freely breathe." It is only natural that the Sumerians should honor the gods whom they served by building great religious temples. These temples were the foci of the Sumerian city-states, and the temple priests controlled much of the land and labor of the city-states' inhabitants. Most important of all, it was in the service of the temples and their gods that the Sumerians made many of their most fundamental contributions to civilization.

The temple buildings themselves constitute humanity's earliest efforts at monumental architecture. Most of them were built on terraced artifical mounds called ziggurats that may have been intended to represent mountains. To the Sumerians, the mountain was the source of the earth's potency and as such constituted an intensely significant religious symbol. The terraced or set-back style of the ziggurat temple and of most other large-scale Mesopotamian architecture was partly dictated by the clay brick that was the chief building material in a land where stone and wood were scarce. The use of clay bricks by Mesopotamian builders also gave rise to such basic architectural forms as the arch.

The first Sumerian writing was done by temple scribes who began to keep accounts of the considerable economic resources that the temples controlled. Such were the mundane beginnings of human literacy. It is quite correct to say, as one writer has done, that "history begins at Sumer," for since history, narrowly speaking, is the reconstruction of the past from written sources, our first strictly historical evidence is Sumerian. The writing of these temple scribes consists of wedge-shaped marks inscribed on clay tablets with a reed stylus. The technique long persisted in Mesopotamia and spread throughout much of the Near East. The script is called *cuneiform* after the Latin *cuneus* which means "wedge." The first cuneiform symbols were pictograms, that is, little pictures of the objects being described. In time, the pictograms evolved into ideograms (conventionalized figures representing things or abstract concepts:. for example, & for *and*). And greater flexibility was gradually achieved by the addition of syllabic symbols (representing phonetic values). Since the cuneiform symbols were exceedingly numerous, writing was a difficult and esoteric art that remained for many centuries the monopoly of a small, highly-trained scribal class.

Sumerian mathematics seems to have arisen also from the

necessities of the temple accounts. Ten was the basic numerical unit among the Sumerians as among so many other peoples, perhaps because the decimal system, so fundamental to mathematics during most ages, is based on the primitive impulse to count on one's fingers. But the Sumerians also stressed units based on the numbers 6, 60, 600, 3600, and so on, which are the source of our present practice of dividing circles into 360°. They understood addition and subtraction, and knew how to handle fractions. They established standard units of weight and measure and devised a lunar calendar. All these achievements were the products of hard, practical necessity, and all appear to have risen first from the needs of the temple community. All, in short, were undertaken for the purpose of better serving the all-powerful gods.

The invention of writing was soon followed by the birth of literature. Here, too, the gods played a dominant role. Religious stories now appeared such as the *Epic of Gilgamish*, a powerful tragedy that describes a Sumerian hero's courageous but fruitless search for immortality and includes an early version of the flood legend. Rich in hymns, prayers, and mythological poetry, Sumerian literature is characterized by a grave, solemn style that scarcely changes at all from one generation to the next. The Sumerian authors and poets saw no value in originality but preferred to follow earlier models and preserve a cherished tradition.

Many of these same qualities are found in Sumerian sculpture. It too was almost exclusively religious, and much of it was devoted to the decoration of the temples. It was executed in a style that by modern standards seems static, somber, and impersonal, and despite a gradual trend toward realism it was nearly as tradition-bound as literature. Yet the statuettes and relief carvings of the Sumerian artists also convey a feeling of dignity—even nobility. Altogether they constitute an admirable expression of the Sumerian religious outlook and take their place alongside the works of the poets and architects as the first expressions of a cultural tradition that was to dominate Western Asia for thousands of years to come.

Figure from Sumerian Temple about 3000 B.C. (*The Metropolitan Museum of Art, Fletcher Fund, 1940*).

**Early Sumerian Politics** | Sumerian society was characterized by a male-dominated hierarchy of priests, nobles, freemen, and peasants. The peasants, who constituted the great majority, were obliged to work the temple lands or the lands of nobles, but they were also given the opportunity to till their own fields and to sell their own surpluses (if any). They were slaves, to be sure, but slaves of the gods, and they shared this condition of servitude with all ranks of society, even nobles and priests. And if all were slaves then, in at least some sense, all were equal. Indeed, most of the Sumerian cities first appear to have been governed by a general assembly of adult males. The practice quickly developed, however, of appointing a temporary king to rule during emergencies. In time, emergencies, actual or contrived, became more frequent until finally monarchy became permanent. As one might expect in such a profoundly religious society as that of Sumer, the chief priest and the king were often the same person. And Sumerian kingship, like almost every other Sumerian institution, was primarily religious in its function. It was the king's task to determine the gods' will by means of dreams or other portents and to carry it out. Even this mighty personage was merely the leading slave of the city's chief god.

During the third millennium numerous city-states occupied the valley, bearing such names as Ur, Lagash, and Uruk. The increasing frequency of emergencies and the concomitant rise of monarchies stemmed largely from the growing tendency toward intercity warfare. The ultimate political unification of the district was long delayed by the fierce independence of the cities. The prisoners taken in the intensified warfare of the epoch became the nucleus of a growing slave class, which had been inconsequential during Mesopotamia's early days.

As the struggles went on, Sumerian civilization spread northward along the Tigris-Euphrates valley into a district called Akkad. This region was settled chiefly by Semitic-speaking peoples who had migrated northward from their original homeland in the Arabian desert. The inhabitants of Akkad soon followed the Sumerian cue, built cities of their own, and joined in the intercity struggle. Thenceforth Meso-

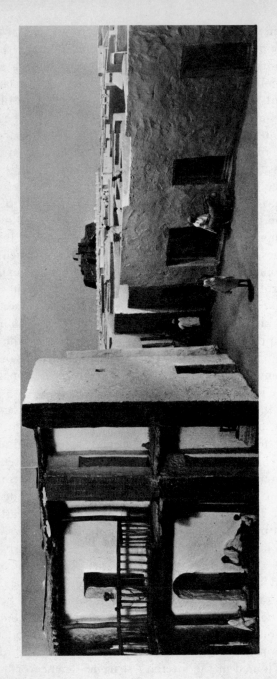

Model of city of Ur, about 2000 B.C. (*courtesy of the American Museum of Natural History*).

potamia was divided between the Semitic northern district of
Akkad and the Sumerian south, usually called Sumer. But the
relationships between Semites and Sumerians were exceedingly complex, and we must not view these peoples simply as
two antagonistic blocks. Occasionally, during the third millennium, a single city would succeed in dominating all Mesopotamia, but its success was usually brief. Sometimes a Sumerian city would gain the ascendency, sometimes an Akkadian city. More than once the area was ruled for a time by an
outside tribe.

**The Political Unification Of Mesopotamia** | The first unifica-
tion of any permanence was accomplished by a Semitic conqueror, the Akkadian king Sargon, who brought Mesopotamia under his rule about 2370 B.C. and whose dynasty
maintained uneasy control for several generations (about
2370–2230). Sargon made a profound impression on his contemporaries, for his empire was the greatest that the Mesopotamian world had ever known. It bound Akkad and Sumer
into a single political unit, and later legend made it even more
extensive than it actually was. Sargon was said to have "reign-
ed over the people of all lands." His conquests had the effect
of accelerating the diffusion of Sumerian culture throughout
the Near East. One of Sargon's successors, breaking with Sumerian tradition, took the step of claiming divinity for himself.

In time, Sargon's Akkadian dynasty was destroyed by in-
vading tribesmen from the northeast whose coming ushered
in another period of political unrest. Around 2100 B.C. the
Sumerian city of Ur rose to dominance (and its kings likewise
claimed divinity), but its empire eventually fell before the
pressures of outside invaders and local particularism. With the
collapse of Ur, Sumerian political power was ended forever.
The future of Mesopotamia lay with the Semites.

During the troubled era around the turn of the millennium
(about 2000 B.C.) several new Semitic peoples were moving
into the valley. One of these tribes, the Amorites from Syria,

occupied several cities, including the obscure town of Babylon. The ablest of the Amorite kings of Babylon, the famous
Hammurabi (about 1792-1750) conquered all of Akkadia
and Sumer and then went on to extend his sway across the
entire Fertile Crescent from the Mediterranean to the Persian
Gulf. Almost overnight Babylon emerged from her former
obscurity to become the capital of an empire.

It must be emphasized that the evidence for these political
developments is thin and ambiguous, and certain details of
our reconstruction may be in error. Our dates in this early
period may be inexact by a century or more. Nevertheless,
the general sequence of events is well established. And there
is little doubt that Hammurabi, building on a Sumerian cultural tradition that had been evolving for nearly 2000 years,
was able to create a political structure of exceptional efficiency. His famous law code serves as a window into daily
life in the Babylonian Empire.

The code was based on a series of earlier, shorter Sumerian
codes and drew heavily from Sumerian custom. Hammurabi
makes no claim to personal divinity but assumes the more
traditional role of steward of the gods. The society that he
rules is stratified into nobles, freemen, and slaves. Detailed
mercantile regulations indicate an active and complex commercial life. But the Code of Hammurabi is noticeably harsh-
er than its Sumerian predecessors, suggesting a higher degree
of authoritarianism than before. Capital punishment is fre-
quent where it had once been rare, and the notion of retribu-
tive justice—an eye for an eye—is carried to macabre ex-
tremes: if a house collapses, killing its occupant, the builder
is executed; if the occupant's son is killed, the builder's son
must die; if a patient dies during an operation, the surgeon is
executed; if the patient loses an eye, the surgeon's fingers are
cut off—a punishment that would prove inconvenient for the
surgeon's future career.

**The Northern Invasions: About 1750 to 1550 B.C.** | Even as
the Babylonian Empire was at its height, the entire Near East

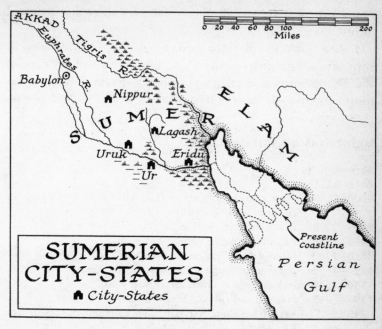

Sumerian City-States.

was being subjected to the pressure of a great series of tribal migrations. New peoples moved down from the mountains of the north and northeast into Mesopotamia, Asia Minor (approximately the modern Turkey), Greece, Crete, and North Africa. They are known collectively as Indo-Europeans, for although they were ethnically diverse, their languages were all derived from a single Indo-European core—the ancestor of Latin, Greek, Persian, Sanskrit, and the Germanic and Romance languages of today (including, of course, English). From the standpoint of language, these newcomers were our own forefathers. Their southward migrations resulted in the violent displacement of other peoples. Between about 1750 and 1550 B.C. they, and others moving in their wake, disrupted the political and cultural continuity of the ancient Near East. In about 1595 Indo-European invaders brought an end to Hammurabi's dynasty in Babylon, plunging Mesopotamia into a long period of cultural decadence and political unrest.

Before moving on into these troubled centuries we will turn our attention from the Tigris-Euphrates to the valley of the Nile where another great civilization was developing almost concurrently with that of Mesopotamia.

## MESOPOTAMIAN CHRONOLOGY

Approximate
Dates B.C.*

| | |
|---|---|
| 4000–2800: | Formation of city-states (formative period of Sumerian culture: c. 3500–2800) |
| 2800–2370: | Era of intercity warfare |
| 2370–2230: | Akkadian Empire: dynasty of Sargon |
| 2230–1790: | Intermediate Era: rise of Babylon |
| 1790–1595: | Babylonian Empire: Hammurabi and Amorites |
| 1750–1550: | Indo-European invasions of Near East |
| 1595– 745: | Political and cultural breakdown |
| 745 ff.: | Era of Empires: Assyrian, Neo-Babylonian, Persian (see Chapter 3) |

*In general, our ancient Near Eastern dating follows the chronology adopted in the *Revised Cambridge Ancient History,* I, Ch. VI.

# 3

## Egypt

**The Setting** | "Egypt is the gift of the Nile." It was the Greek historian Herodotus who made this observation, but its truth had long before been recognized by the Egyptians themselves. One of their most moving hymns opens with these words: "Hail to thee, O Nile, that issues from the earth and comes to keep Egypt alive!"*

The valley of the Nile winds northward like a green serpent through the barren North African desert, spreading out as it approaches the Mediterranean into a vast flat delta. The narrow valley to the south and the delta to the north form two distinct regions known as Upper and Lower Egypt. (Since the two regions are named according to their location on the northward flowing Nile, Lower Egypt will be *above* Upper Egypt on a modern map.) Therefore, ancient Egypt has been called "the Kingdom of the Two Lands."

**The Formative Period: About 3250 to 2700 B.C.** | The remarkable fertility of the Nile valley, like that of the Tigris-

*J. B. Pritchard, ed., *Ancient Near Eastern Texts* (Princeton, 1950), p. 372.

Euphrates, resulted from the rich silt deposited by annual floods. The evolution from Neolithic culture to civilization in Egypt more or less followed the pattern established in Mesopotamia: swamps were drained, junglelike vegetation was cleared, and canals were dug, so that the fecundity of the black land could be exploited. Indeed, the presence of Sumerian artifacts and artistic motifs from the beginning of this formative period suggests a Mesopotamian influence in Egypt's rise to civilization. An ancient Mesopotamian knife, for example, has been discovered in the Wadi Hammamat, near the Nile, and the early Egyptian step pyramids bear a certain resemblance to the Mesopotamian Ziggurats.

Toward the close of the fourth millennium, the Nile valley was divided into political units called "nomes." Gradually these nomes seem to have coalesced into larger units, and around 3100 B.C. a great conqueror from Upper Egypt named Narmer (or Menes) unified the entire land, established a capital at Memphis, and became the first of the pharaohs.

The next 400 years or so constitute an intensely creative epoch in Egyptian history. Between about 3100 and 2700, while the early pharaohs were consolidating their authority, a culture was developing that would orient Egyptian life for the next two millennia. The irrigation system was vastly expanded. An extensive knowledge of observational astronomy was put to use in the development of a 365-day solar calendar, far more efficient than the lunar calendar of the Mesopotamians. Important work was done in physiology and medicine that would not be surpassed until the time of the Greeks. A graceful, majestic artistic style evolved, and architects were showing increasing skill in designing large structures of stone. Hieroglyphic writing, already known in 3100, was being developed into a literary vehicle. This was an exciting, adventurous period of artistic and cultural experimentation. At its close in about 2700, Egyptian civilization had reached maturity. It is well to pause here, at the end of Egypt's adolescence, to examine the ethos that was taking form.

Ancient Egypt.

**Environment And Outlook** | Although both Egypt and Meso-
potamia arose out of the taming of river valleys, the two civilizations differed sharply in style and mood, in part because
they differed in environment. The Nile valley was far kinder
to its inhabitants than was the Valley of the Two Rivers. The
Nile floods might occasionally elude human control, and
there were lean years in Egypt as well as abundant ones, yet,
on the whole, the Egyptian environment was beneficent. The
flooding Nile raged less savagely than the Tigris-Euphrates.
The winds were softer and the sky clearer. In contrast to
present-day Egypt, the population of the Nile valley in antiquity was relatively small and the natural resources of the
area were usually sufficient to support it. Finally, the surrounding deserts tended to protect Egyptian civilization, especially in its earlier phases, from the incessant invasions that
afflicted Mesopotamia. There was an amiable regularity to
the Egyptian environment, and the forces of nature seemed
comparatively docile.

Accordingly, the ancient Egyptians tended to be confident, pragmatic, and optimistic. They were convinced that
nature had blessed them and would continue to do so—that
they were a singularly favored people. Above all, they possessed a sense of security lacking among the Mesopotamians.
Of course individuals differ, and early Egypt doubtless had its
pessimists just as Mesopotamia had its optimists, but the
mood expressed by early Egyptian art, architecture, and literature is one of serenity and confidence—often even gaiety and
vivaciousness. There is an emphasis on material values—on the
good things of this world and the pleasures of the moment.

Once established, Egyptian culture and Egyptian society
changed little over the centuries. This conservatism was by no
means absolute, for the Egyptian spirit was sufficiently tolerant and undogmatic to accept such cultural adjustments as
changing conditions might require. Yet by the standards of
later civilizations, Egypt was remarkably static. Her inertia
was in part a product of her isolation, but it stemmed also
from the attitude of the Egyptians themselves. Theirs seemed

the best of all possible worlds, and their impulse was to perpetuate rather than change it. They hoped, indeed they confidently expected, that the future would be an endless extension of the present.

The Egyptian preoccupation with the afterlife, often regarded as morbid, seems actually to have been a variation on this same theme—a bold assertion that the basic realities of the present would last forever in both this world and the next. It was not an unhealthy obsession with death but a confident affirmation of life.

**Ma'at And The Pharaoh** | The Egyptians responded to nature's favor by viewing the universe as orderly and benevolent. The key concept in Egyptian religious thought is expressed in the word *ma'at,* which may be translated variously as "truth," "justice," "harmony," "balance," or "righteousness." The gods were not ferocious and arbitrary as in Mesopotamia, nor were the Egyptians their slaves. On the contrary, the gods cared about Egypt and favored it exceedingly. Indeed, the pharaoh himself was a living god and his rule was, at least ideally, a perfect manifestation of *ma'at.* All Egypt was his personal estate, and his slightest whim was law. Egypt produced no law codes as Mesopotamia did, for the law was in the pharaoh's mouth. Yet, being a god, he expressed in his words and deeds the basic harmony of the cosmos. He was the divine and victorious champion of the Egyptians against the forces of chaos and darkness.

The potency of the god-king concept affected every aspect of ancient Egyptian life. The great early works of monumental architecture were royal tombs rather than temples (although temple architecture became significant in the later phases of the civilization). Most of the early sculpture and decorative art was associated with the tombs of the pharaohs. Every Egyptian was subject to the pharaoh's orders. Each was obliged to give a high proportion of his produce to the royal treasury and could be drafted for personal service on the royal tombs or in the royal mines. The pharaoh possessed a monopoly of foreign trade, and exercised a high degree of control over the entire Egyptian economy.

Yet this king-centered system did not break the spirit of the individual Egyptian. Peasants are shown in the tomb scenes singing at their work. There was opportunity for men of ability to rise and prosper in the pharaoh's service. It is perhaps going too far to suggest, as one enthusiastic scholar has done, that the pyramids themselves were vast public works projects. But one does get the impression that the rule of the god-king was accepted gratefully, not sullenly; Egyptian history is almost entirely free of lower-class rebellions.

**Religious Thought** | Like other ancient peoples, the Egyptians crowded their universe with gods and spirits. Their greatest god, Re, personified the life-giving sun. He appeared in many guises and was often merged with some local god into a kind of divine compound. Amon-Re became in middle and later Egyptian history the most illustrious of these compound gods. During the empire period, Amon-Re was god of victories and his magnificent temple at Karnak became unimaginably wealthy.

Osiris, another important deity, was said to have once been a great and benevolent pharaoh. His sister-wife Isis was believed to have been supremely wise and adept at the arts of magic. Later legend declared that Osiris had been killed by his brother but, owing to the lamentations of Isis, was miraculously resurrected. Osiris afterwards passed on into the next world to become the judge of souls. This theme of death and resurrection was basic to ancient religious thought. A mythological expression of the death of vegetation in winter and its resurrection in spring, the concept also symbolized the death of the sun each evening and its rebirth at dawn. Indeed, the Nile itself followed this same sequence; the low Nile of early spring, bringing the specter of famine to the land, gave way each summer to a new, resurgent Nile that revivified the fields. And the individual Egyptian might well hope that he too, like the sun and the river, would conquer death. The Osiris-Isis myth eventually came to symbolize this hope of individual salvation and eternal life. It remained an important mystery cult in Hellenistic and Roman times.

The pharaoh himself was identified with the god Horus, the son of Isis and Osiris, but he also claimed to be the son of Re. This illogical situation is typical of Egyptian religious thought which was a luxuriant growth filled with contradictions. Its glaring incongruities were cheerfully accepted by the tolerant Egyptian whose religious orientation was mythological and poetic rather than systematic.

**The Old Kingdom: About 2700 to 2200 B.C.** | The coming of age of Egyptian civilization was followed by a 500-year period known as the Old Kingdom (2700-2200 B.C.) during which Egyptian culture flourished under the power of the pharaohs and the favor of the gods. The Old Kingdom was Egypt's classical age. At no other time was Egypt so stable or so confident. The authority and prestige of the pharaohs of this period are illustrated dramatically by the pyramids erected during the fourth dynasty (about 2650-2500 B.C.). The Great Pyramid of Khufu (or Cheops: about 2600) is a staggering mass of more than six million tons of stone fitted together with the percision of a watchmaker—a testimony not only to the patience and craftsmanship of its builders but also to their knowledge of practical mathematics. The pyramids were built without tackle, pulleys, cranes, or wheeled vehicles (the wheel had not yet come to Egypt). The cost in human labor must have been prodigious, yet we need not regard the pyramids as brutal monuments to the ego of the pharaohs whose tombs they were. The pharaoh, the god-king, was the nexus of Egyptian religious thought, and his tomb was a kind of national religious monument. The proper entombment of the dead pharaoh was essential, so it was believed, to the perpetuation of *ma'at* and the continued prosperity of the kingdom.

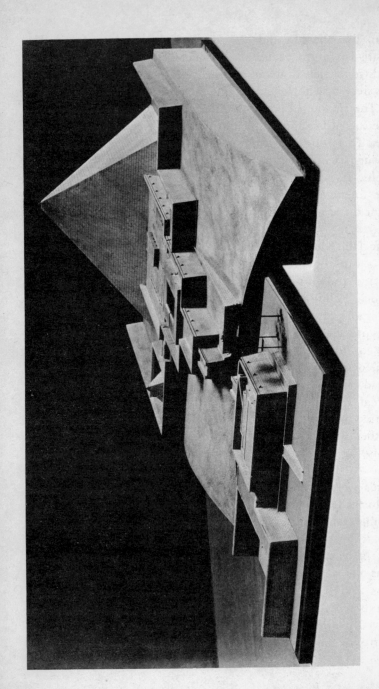

Model of Great Pyramid complex (*The Metropolitan Museum of Art, Dodge Fund, 1911*).

**The First Intermediate Period: About 2200 to 2050 B.C.** | As
the Old Kingdom drew to its end, the power and majesty of
the pharaoh began to wane while the status of the priesthood
and nobility rose. The nomarchs, who served as the pharaoh's
agents in the provinces or nomes, became increasingly auton-
omous. Around 2200 the authority of the pharaoh was
eclipsed altogether, and the nomarchs became the real masters of the land. The era of unrest and particularism that followed is known as the First Intermediate Period. The breakdown was purely internal, brought about by excessive delega-
tion of royal rights and by the ever-increasing burden of
building and maintaining the stupendous royal tombs.
Egypt's isolation continued to shelter her from external dangers; like the imaginary kingdom of Oz, the Egyptian monarchy was protected by a deadly desert from every threat
except that of the nomes.

The collapse of royal authority with its concomitant social upheaval was a devastating blow to Egyptian confidence.
The more sensitive spirits of the age bemoaned the loss of
*ma'at*. Some wrote of the advantages of suicide; others lost
themselves in wine, women, and song. One writer complains,
"I show you the land topsy-turvy. That which never happened has happened. Men take up weapons of warfare, so that
the land lives in confusion . . ."*

But the general Egyptian reaction to this disaster was neither cynicism nor despair. It was a serious effort to replace
the old materialistic values of the past with deeper spiritual
and moral values. Eternal life had formerly been associated
with huge tombs and limited to the pharaoh and his immediate followers. Now salvation was made to depend more upon
an upright life than an appropriate tomb, and the possibility
of an after life was extended to nobles and commoners.
Eternity was democratized.

---

*Quoted in John A. Wilson, *The Culture of Ancient Egypt* (Chicago, 1951), p.
107.

This new cosmic egalitarianism affected Egyptian thought and society in a hundred different ways. A text from the First Intermediate Period has the creator god say, "I made the four winds that every man might breathe thereof . . . I made the great inundation that the poor man might have rights therein like the great man . . . I made every man like his fellow."* For the first time in human history, long before the age of the socially conscious Hebrew prophets, Egypt glimpsed the doctrine of human dignity and justice for the individual. The rulers of society were enjoined to treat their people righteously or else forfeit eternal life.

**The Middle Kingdom: About 2050 to 1800 B.C.** | Gradually, the pharaohs recovered something of their former position, and with this revival of royal power the Middle Kingdom began. A new capital was established at Thebes in Upper Egypt. The former confidence and sense of special election returned; the doctrine of the god-king persisted. Even the old materialism and optimism were reasserted. But they were tempered by the social conscience that Egypt had newly acquired. From our own viewpoint it is one of the tragedies of Egyptian history that as the Middle Kingdom prospered the impulse toward a recognition of human dignity gradually waned and finally disappeared. The vision was daring and unprecedented, but it did not last.

Nor did the monarchy rule with its former absolute authority. The nomarchs remained powerful, and the priesthood grew richer and stronger. But art and literature flourished once more, always within the framework of ideas and forms established during the first dynasties of the Old Kingdom. Egyptian cultural influences and commercial relationships now spread far beyond the Nile valley. And the tomb scenes show the same gaiety and humor as before.

*Quoted in John A. Wilson, *The Culture of Ancient Egypt* (Chicago, 1951), p. 117.

**The Second Intermediate Period: About 1800 to 1550 B.C.** |
We have seen that the Indo-European invasions of about
1750 to 1550 B.C. brought chaos to Mesopotamia in the
wake of Hammurabi's empire. These same invasions exerted
an indirect influence upon Egypt. By driving other peoples
from their lands, the Indo-Europeans started a chain reaction
which created strong external pressure against the Nile valley.
Incursion from without, together with renewed internal problems, brought an end to the Middle Kingdom and led to a
Second Intermediate Period (about 1880–1550 B.C.). Between about 1720 and 1570 Egypt actually fell under the
control of an external people. These conquerors, the Hyksos,
were not themselves Indo-Europeans. Rather they were a
mixed people from Palestine, Syria, and Asia Minor—chiefly
Semitic in language and culture—whose migrations were a
part of the general upheaval that the Indo-European invasions
brought about. Although the influence of the Hyksos in
Egyptian life was limited primarily to the collection of tribute, they demolished for all time the feeling of confidence
and buoyancy which Egypt's former isolation had fostered.
The continuity of Egyptian culture was by no means ended,
but it was seriously compromised. Thereafter Egypt was
never quite the same.

**The New Kingdom: About 1550 to 1150 B.C.** | The Hyksos
brought the horse and the chariot into Egypt and introduced
new military techniques. Egypt learned, and in time was able
to use the new military technology against the Hyksos themselves, driving them out of the land around 1570 B.C. Then
for a third time the monarchy reasserted itself, and the New
Kingdom came into being.

After about a century of consolidation (about 1550–1465)
the pharaohs began to pursue a policy of overt imperialism,
leading large armies out of a land that had once known only
small police forces and militia. With remarkable speed the
Egyptians conquered a large, profitable empire that included
the rich provinces of Syria and Palestine. Egypt's age of innocence was over at last, and the valley was now open not only

to new luxuries but also to new styles, new ideas, and new religions.

The intellectual and artistic currents of this cosmopolitan age wrought a violent transformation in the Egyptian mood. The old serenity gave way to an exciting, fluid, occasionally nervous style. The old idealized portraiture gave way to extreme realism, even caricature and an obsession with the grotesque. The empire was maintained only at the cost of constant watchfulness and ever-increasing tension, and the old sense of confidence and optimism, shattered by the Hyksos, did not return. The social conscience of the First Intermediate Period and early Middle Kingdom was beyond recovery in the highly regimented society that the burden of empire made necessary. Yet, despite the new regimentation and sharp social stratification, the pharaoh was no longer the divine autocrat that the Old Kingdom had known. His independence and authority were increasingly compromised by the rise of priestly power and his wealth was rivaled by that of the god Amon-Re.

**Akhnaton: About 1379 To 1361 B.C.** | Etched against this fluctuating background is the tragic figure of the pharaoh Akhnaton, who has been called mankind's first monotheist. Akhnaton deliberately rejected the many gods whom Egyptians had habitually worshipped. He defied the powerful priesthood of Amon-Re, suppressed the cult of Osiris, and effaced the names of these and other gods from the temples. In Their place Akhnaton proclaimed a new god, the Aton, who is represented in the art of the period by a solar disc with rays extending outward ending in hands. The Aton was god of all men—god of the universe. His essence was *ma'at:* "truth." He was the creator of the world, for Akhnaton himself declares in his famous hymn to the Aton:

> O sole god, like whom there is no other!
> Thou didst create the world according to thy desire,
> Whilst thou wert alone.*

*Tr. J. A. Wilson, in J. B. Pritchard, ed., *The Ancient Near East* (Princeton, 1958), p. 229.

225

Akhnaton worshiping the Aton (*Art Reference Bureau—Cairo Museum*).

Akhnaton's theological revolution must be understood as part of the new imperial age. For one thing, it was an attempt to destroy the ever-increasing power of the established priesthoods, especially that of Amon-Re. For another, the Aton's universalism symbolizes the new cosmopolitanism of a people whose world was no longer bounded by the valley of the Nile. And in the art associated with Akhnaton and his court, the fluid, realistic style of the Empire reached a crescendo. Yet Akhnaton was himself no imperialist, for the Empire was allowed to crumble during his reign and had to be rebuilt by his successors.

The worship of the Aton scarcely survived Akhnaton's death, although the new artistic tendencies continued to flourish. Within a few years the bold heresy had been demolished, and Osiris and Amon-Re returned in triumph. Why did Akhnaton fail? Doubtless there were many reasons, but perhaps the most significant is the nature of the Aton himself. He was a cold and distant deity, a god of the intellect rather than the emotions. Nor was he really the only god, for Akhnaton, in good Egyptian tradition, regarded himself as divine. Indeed, in Akhnaton's system only the pharaoh and his family worshipped the Aton. Everybody else worshipped the pharaoh. "Thou art in my heart," says Akhnaton to his god, "And there is no other that knows thee."* Consequently the Aton had no real impact on Egypt at large even during Akhnaton's reign. The theory that Akhnaton's religious ideas influenced the Hebrews who were then slaves in Egypt, thereby propelling Israel toward monotheism, seems most unlikely. But whatever its weaknesses, Akhnaton's vision was of singular nobility and breadth. If he fell short of monotheism, he approached it more closely than anyone before him.

Conclusion | The empire, which survived Akhnaton's death by two centuries, ultimately succumbed to another great wave of invasions that disrupted the Near East between about

*Ibid., p. 230.

1200 and 900 B.C. Thereafter Egypt was ruled for the most part by foreign dynasties or foreign peoples, Libyan, Assyrian, Persian, Greek, and Roman. During the intervals between these periods of foreign domination the Egyptians sought to recapture their earlier creative spirit, but it always eluded them. The forms of the past were repeated endlessly but the spirit of the past was beyond recovery.

Egyptian civilization ended ingloriously, as perhaps all civilizations must, but it had remained vigorous for two thousand years. The Egyptians failed to achieve eternity as they had hoped, but they came closer to doing so than any other people. And although their dynamism was exhausted at last, their art and architecture, their science and medicine, even their religion, became the legacy of newer cultures. The Greek column is Egyptian in origin, and the Greeks were honest enough to admit their debt to Egypt in science, medicine, and mathematics. Above all, the Egyptians, together with the Sumerians, were the creators of civilization itself. Israel and Persia, Greece and Rome, were built on their ruins.

### EGYPTIAN CHRONOLOGY

Approximate
Dates B. C.

| | |
|---|---|
| 3250 ff.: | Era of Mesopotamian influence |
| 3100—2700: | First dynasties: cultural adolescence |
| 2700—2200: | Old Kingdom (Great Pyramids: c. 2650—2500) |
| 2200—2050: | First Intermediate Period |
| 2050—1800: | Middle Kingdom |
| 1800—1550: | Second Intermediate Period (Hyksos domination: c. 1720—1570) |
| 1750—1550: | Indo-European invasions of Near East |
| 1550—1150: | New Kingdom (Empire: c. 1480—1165; Akhnaton: 1379—1361) |
| 1150 ff.: | Post-Empire Period |

# 4

## The Diffusion of
## Near Eastern
## Civilization

**The Indo-European Invasions: About 1750 to 1550; About 1200 to 900** | As large portions of the ancient Near East were brought under control of great empires such as those of Sargon, Hammurabi, and the Egyptians, the influence of Mesopotamian and Egyptian culture spread throughout the Fertile Crescent and beyond. By the second millennium the whole Near East had become a vast cultural melting pot. But the unifying impulse represented by these successive imperialistic efforts was countered by the shattering effects of repeated invasions from the north. We have seen that the first great wave of Indo-European invaders reached its peak between 1750 and 1550. After 1550 the Indo-European pressure diminished but it did not end. On the contrary, after a time it began to increase once more, reaching a second climax between 1200 and 900.

The political and cultural history of the second millennium must be understood in the context of these two great irruptions. The first, as we have seen, contributed to the decline of Hammurabi's Babylonian Empire and the collapse of the

Egyptian Middle Kingdom. During the interlude between the two invasions Babylonia remained in the doldrums, but several vigorous cultures flourished to the north and west. One of these, the Egyptian Empire, has already been discussed. Another, the Minoan-Mycenaean civilization centering on the Aegean Sea, will be treated in the next chapter because of its relevance to the subsequent rise of the Greeks. Still another kingdom, established in Asia Minor (modern Turkey) by a group of Indo-European invaders known as Hittites, struggled with the Egyptian Empire for control of Syria. The kingdom of the Hittites reached its height in the fourteenth century, at the time when Egypt was preoccupied with Akhnaton's religious reforms.

Between 1200 and 900 B.C., the political structure of the inter-invasion epoch was brought down in ruins by the second great wave of Indo-European invaders. The Hittite Empire and the Minoan-Mycenaean culture were destroyed altogether, and Egypt retired in exhaustion to the shelter of the Nile valley. This was the age when the Celts invaded western Europe, the Latins (the later Romans) settled in central Italy, and the Dorian Greeks (among whom were the later Spartans) moved southward to ravage the cities of earlier Greek settlers.

These invasions were concurrent with the coming of the Iron Age. Since iron smelting was more complicated than copper production, the peoples of the Near East did not discover the uses of iron until well after they had learned how to produce copper. The Hittites seem to have pioneered in iron production, but it was not until the disorders following about 1200 that iron technology became widely known in southern Europe and the Near East. In the wake of the invasions, iron tools and weapons spread quickly throughout the ancient world not only because of the intrinsic superiority of iron to bronze, but also because of its far greater abundance. The sharply increased availability of metal that resulted from this "iron revolution" had a profoundly democratizing effect; the Bronze Age aristocracies lost their monopoly on metal as iron weapons and tools came more and more into the hands of commoners.

The Canaanites | The turbulent centuries between about 1200 and 900 presented a unique opportunity to the small Semitic tribes of Syria and Palestine whose lands had hitherto been a battleground of empires. Now the great inter-invasion states were either dead or dormant, and the territories along the eastern shore of the Mediterranean came into their own at last.

The dominant people in Syria-Palestine around the middle of the second millennium were known as Canaanites. Their culture, with its roots in both Mesopotamia and Egypt, was generally derivative, but they made one original contribution of tremendous significance: the development of the first true alphabet. In place of the hundreds of syllabic signs of the earlier scripts, the Canaanites used twenty-nine symbols representing the consonants. The alphabet was reduced later on to twenty-two letters, and still later the Greeks added vowels. But even without these improvements the Canaanite alphabet constituted an enormous simplification and opened up the possibility of a vast expansion of literacy. Writing was never again the mysterious art that it had formerly been, and the monopoly of the old scribal class was doomed. Like the coming of iron, the invention of the alphabet extended the benefits of civilization to a much larger segment of society than ever before.

The city-states of the Canaanites were subjected to devastating attacks between 1300 and 1000, first by the Israelites who had crossed the Sinai Desert from Egypt and later by the Philistines, one of the "sea peoples" whose invasions wrought such havoc throughout the Near East. The Canaanites lost much of their territory but were able to maintain control of a narrow coastal strip known as Phoenicia.

The Phoenicians, as these later Canaanites were called, had a remarkable talent for commerce. Independent Phoenician cities, such as Sidon and Tyre, sent their ships throughout the

Mediterranean and served the function of cultural middlemen between the Near East and Europe. The Greek language, for example, is written in an alphabet adapted from the Phoenician. Phoenician merchants sailed westward through the Straits of Gibraltar into the Atlantic perhaps as far as Britain and the Azores, and down the west coast of Africa to Cape Verde. The greatest of the many Phoenician trading bases was Carthage, founded by Tyre late in the eighth century and destined to acquire wealth and power far beyond the dreams of the Phoenicians themselves.

**The Israelites** | No other ancient Near Eastern people are as familiar to us as the Israelites. Their Bible has been studied by scholars and men of faith throughout the centuries of Western civilization. It is the fountainhead of Judaism, Islam, and Christianity, and a crucial element in the heritage of modern peoples. As a historical source it enables us to endow the dry bones of ancient Israel with flesh and life. But it also raises serious problems of historical criticism. The Biblical critics of the nineteenth century rejected the traditional belief in divine inspiration and subjected the Bible to painstaking scrutiny of the sort that historians normally apply to their documents. These critics doubted the historical existence of Abraham, Jacob—even Moses—and concluded that the Bible was not especially good history. More recently, however, certain Biblical episodes that were previously rejected as mere myth have been corroborated by new archaeological discoveries and by comparisons with non-Biblical sources. Scholars are now inclined to regard the Bible as a relatively reliable body of ancient historical documents.

According to the Bible, the history of the Jews begins when the patriarch Abraham entered into an agreement or *Covenant* with a specific deity, "the God of Abraham." Abraham promised not to recognize or worship any other god, and, in return, he and his family were taken under the special protection of the God of Abraham. The Covenant was renewed by all succeeding generations of Abraham's clan and became a basic ingredient of Jewish religious thought. It seems unlikely that Abraham viewed his God as the only god. Had he been asked, he would doubtless have conceded the existence of other deities, yet from the *practical* standpoint even Abraham was a monotheist. The existence of other gods was irrelevant to him, for it was his God alone that Abraham honored.

Under Jacob, Abraham's grandson, the clan is said to have been driven by famine from Palestine to Egypt. This migration probably occurred sometime around 1600 B.C.—toward the end of the Hyksos regime. It was probably not limited to Jacob and his immediate family but included kindred folk who would be known henceforth as Hebrews. The Hebrews seem to have prospered in Egypt during the Hyksos epoch, but when the Egyptians expelled the Hyksos around 1570 they enslaved all remaining foreigners, forcing them to labor for the state. During this prolonged period of bondage, the Covenant of Abraham was extended to include more and more of the Hebrews. In the meantime the Egyptian Empire rose, and Akhnaton experimented with his remarkable solar religion. But the Hebrews, at the bottom of the Egyptian social order, were essentially unaffected.

At length, perhaps sometime in the fourteenth century, a Hebrew, trained in the Egyptian bureaucracy and bearing the Egyptian name of Moses, led a band of his own and other enslaved peoples to freedom. For a long generation they wandered in the Wilderness of the Sinai Desert. Under Moses' superb leadership they were forged into a unified people and the personal Covenant was transformed into a Covenant between God and the whole Hebrew nation. The God of Abraham was given the name "Yahweh" (traditionally translated as Jehovah). It is to this Sinai period that the Bible ascribes the divine dictation of the Ten Commandments.

Moses had promised to lead his people to the "promised land" of Palestine or Canaan. But when the Hebrews emerged at last from the wilderness, Moses was dead, and a new generation had arisen. Under the leadership of Joshua, the Hebrews entered the land of the Canaanites, perhaps around the beginning of the thirteenth century, and won a series of important victories. The best known of Joshua's battles was fought at the ancient city of Jericho whose walls, we are told, came tumbling down. But the struggle with the Canaanites did not end with these initial battles. It continued with many ups and downs for another two centuries during which the Hebrews were deeply influenced by Canaanite civilization. They adopted a Canaanite dialect and used the Canaanite alphabet. Some even began to worship Canaanite gods, much to the chagrin of the orthodox. During these centuries the Hebrews were loosely organized into tribes under local military leaders known inappropriately as "judges." The epoch of the judges gave way at length to a unified monarchy which was made necessary by the increasing military pressure of an aggressive tribe of invaders: the Philistines.

**The United Israelite Kingdom and Its Aftermath** | In 1020, the priest Samuel anointed Saul, Israel's first king. Saul waged war against the Philistines with some success but was far outshone by his able successor, David (1005 to 965), who is said to have demonstrated his prowess even as a child by slaying the great Philistine, Goliath, with a slingshot. Under David and his son Solomon (965–925), Israel reached its political zenith. Their kingdom was the most powerful in the ancient history of Syria-Palestine, dominating the entire area and extending far inland toward the Euphrates. Phoenicia retained its independence only through a policy of submissive cooperation. This was the golden age that etched itself on Israel's imagination for all time to come—the age that for endless generations the Jews never despaired of recovering.

It was David's great hope to build a permanent, central temple for Yahweh in Jerusalem, a city that he had recently conquered, and under Solomon the temple was completed. Jerusalem itself became the cosmopolitan capital of a wealthy empire. Solomon surrounded himself with all the trappings of Near Eastern monarchy from bureaucrats to concubines. But

Solomon's subjects were obliged to pay for all this imperial glory with heavy taxes and forced labor, and many of them concluded that the price was too high. Upon Solomon's death (925 B.C.) Israelite particularism reasserted itself, and the kingdom broke into two halves: a large state to the north known thenceforth as Israel, and the smaller and more unified state of Judah to the south, centering on Jerusalem.

This political split brought an early end to Hebrew imperialism. With the close of the second epoch of Indo-European invasions around 900 B.C., the Near East entered a new age of great empires. The first of these, the Assyrian Empire, exerted increasing military pressure against both Israel and Judah. Israel fell to the Assyrians in 722, and her people were scattered across the Near East where they faded into the indigenous populations and vanished from history. Judah survived the Assyrian attacks only to fall to Assyria's imperial successor, the New Babylonian Empire, in 586. Judah's political and intellectual leaders were banished to Babylon where they and their children endured that tragic epoch in Biblical history, the Babylonian Captivity (586–539 B.C.). The bitterness of exile is captured in the opening lines of the 137th Psalm:

> By the rivers of Babylon,
> There we sat down, yea, we wept,
> When we remembered Zion.

**The Prophets** | The devastating experience of divided kingdom and Babylonian Captivity evoked a profound religious response. During these years the moral initiative passed from kings and priests to inspired individuals known as prophets, whose boldly original spiritual insights—arising out of an age of despair—deepened and ennobled the Hebrew religion. To the prophets, law and ritual were insufficient without sincerity of purpose and righteousness of life. The prophet Micah expressed this insight with striking brevity:

> It has been shown to you, O man, what is good
>     and what the Lord requires of you:

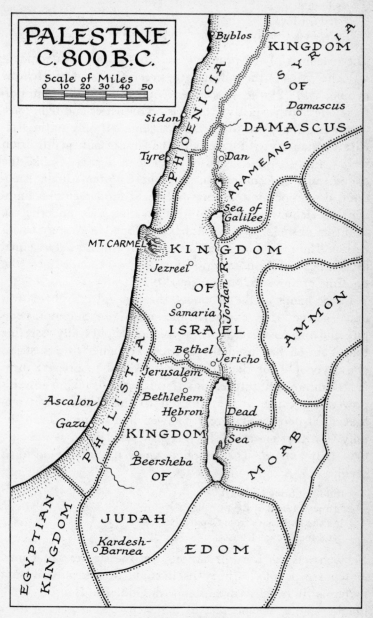

## PALESTINE C. 800 B.C.

Scale of Miles
0   10   20   30   40   50

*Byblos*

KINGDOM

*PHOENICIA*

*SYRIA*

OF

*Damascus*

*Sidon*

DAMASCUS

*Tyre*

*Dan*

*ARAMEANS*

*Sea of Galilee*

MT. CARMEL

KINGDOM

*Jezreel*

OF

*Jordan R.*

AMMON

*Samaria*

ISRAEL

*Bethel*

*Jericho*

*Jerusalem*

*Ascalon*

*Bethlehem*

*Gaza*

*Hebron*

*Dead*

KINGDOM

*Sea*

*Beersheba*

OF

MOAB

PHILISTIA

EGYPTIAN KINGDOM

JUDAH

*Kardesh-Barnea*

EDOM

Palestine, 800 B.C.

> Only to do justice
> and live loyally
> and walk humbly with your God [6:8].

The teachings of the prophets were based on two fundamental concepts: (1) the covenant between God and his Hebrew people, and (2) the consequent obligation of Israelites to treat one another justly. Their vision of justice and righteousness was not applied to mankind at large but only to the Israelite community; yet even with that important qualification it was a profound affirmation of human dignity. Unlike the ephemeral social consciousness of the Egyptian Middle Kingdom, the prophetic teachings became a fundamental component of Hebrew thought. More than that, they underlie the tradition of social justice that has developed in Western Civilization. The prophets' insistence that all Israelites were equal in the sight of God would ultimately be expanded into the doctrine of universal human equality.

In the hands of the prophets, the concept of Yahweh was universalized. They explained the collapse of Solomon's empire and the Assyrian and Babylonian conquests by asserting that Yahweh had used the Hebrews' enemies to punish his chosen people for their transgressions and to prepare them for a triumphant future. But if this was so, then Yahweh's power was evidently not limited to the Hebrews but embraced all peoples. Whereas Yahweh had formerly been the only God that *mattered*, he was now proclaimed as the only God that *existed*. The prophet Amos quotes the Lord as saying,

> Did I not bring up Israel
> from the land of Egypt
> and the Philistines from Caphtor
> and the Syrians from Kir? [9:7].

Yahweh was the Lord of nations, yet the Hebrews remained his chosen people. History itself could be understood only in terms of Israel's encounter with God. The Hebrews were unique among the peoples of the ancient Near East in their sensitivity toward history, for to them God's relations with man occurred in a historical dimension, and history itself was directed by God toward certain predetermined goals. Thus, it was Yahweh, not the Babylonians, who sent the Hebrews into exile, and in the fullness of time, so the prophets said, Yahweh would build their kingdom anew. A divinely appointed leader of the house of David—a Messiah—would one day be sent to consummate the divine plan by reestablishing the political glory of Israel. This assurance helped the Hebrew exiles preserve their integrity and their faith against the lures of a powerful alien culture. For although many succumbed to the temptations of Babylon, others held fast in the conviction that history was on their side.

**Later Jewish History** | In 539 B.C. the New Babylonian Empire gave way to the Persian Empire, and the Hebrews were permitted to return to their homeland and rebuild the temple of Jerusalem. They could now practice their faith without interference, but they remained under Persian political control. Two centuries thereafter Persian rule gave way to Greek rule, and in time the Greeks were replaced by the Romans. During these post-exilic centuries, the Hebrew sacred writings were collected, sifted, and expanded, and the Old Testament acquired its final form.

As always, the Israelites were torn between the desire to preserve the purity of their heritage and the impulse to accommodate themselves to outside cultural influences. From time to time they rebelled against their political masters but never with lasting success. A Hebrew rebellion in A.D. 70 prompted the Romans to destroy their temple and scatter them throughout the Empire. There followed an exile far more prolonged than the earlier ones in Egypt and Babylonia, lasting until the present century. But the Jews had demonstrated long before that they could survive as a people and a faith without political unity.

The impact of the ancient Hebrews on future civilizations has been immense. The Old Testament, a tremendous literary monument in and of itself, has been of incalculable impor-

tance in the development of European culture. The Hebrews'
sense of history—as a dynamic, purposive, morally-significant
process of human-divine interaction—went far beyond the
historical concepts of other Near Eastern peoples and became
a fundamental element in the historical vision of Western
Civilization. But at the core of everything is their ethical
monotheism—their vision of a single God of infinite power
who is also a God of righteousness and mercy. The Hebrew
confronted his universe in a new way. The world was no
longer pregnant with spirits; nature was no longer a "Thou,"
but rather the handiwork of a far greater "Thou." The myr-
iad spooks and demons of tree, rock, and mountain dissolved
before the unutterable holiness of the God of Israel.

**The Post-Invasion Empires: Assyrians and Chaldeans: About
745 to 539 B.C.** | The last phase of ancient Near Eastern his-
tory runs from the end of the second Indo-European invasion, around 900 B.C., to the conquest of the Persian Empire
by the Greeks under Alexander the Great in 330 B.C. During
these centuries Near Eastern imperialism reached its zenith.
The first of the great post-invasion empires was carved out by
the Assyrians, a warlike Semitic people from northern Mesopotamia who dominated the Near East through a policy of
ruthless militarism. The Assyrians had long been a power in
the Near East, but they reached their height in the years between 745 and 612, exerting their cruel dominion over all
Western Asia and even ruling Egypt for a brief period. The
entire ancient world was momentarily united under a power
that terrorized its subjects and crushed insurrections with
fearful severity. One Assyrian king boasted of punishing a
group of rebels by tearing out their tongues, mashing them
alive, and feeding their corpses to pigs and vultures.

Assyrian culture was Sumerian in inspiration. Its gods were
similar to those of Sumer and Akkad although much more
warlike. The Assyrian king, in good Sumerian tradition, was
viewed as the human representative of the chief god, but his
prestige was much higher than that of his Mesopotamian

Assyrian Empire, 625 B.C.

predecessors. The supreme expression of Assyrian architecture, for example, was the royal palace, not the temple.

Assyrian militarism brought unity and even a degree of peace and prosperity to the long-troubled Near East, but it was a peace based on terror. Once Assyrian leadership faltered, the Empire collapsed before the rage of its subject peoples. A coalition of Indo-European Medes from Iran and Semitic Chaldeans from Babylonia destroyed the power of Assyria for all time to come. The Assyrian capital of Nineveh fell in 612 B.C., and its site remains desolate to this day.

Between the fall of Assyria and the rise of Persia (about 612–539 B.C.) the Near East was divided among several powers. Egypt had already recovered its independence. Anatolia fell under the control of the Lydians, a people who gave

Lydian coins, 560 to 540 B.C. (*The American Museum of Art, Gift of the American Society for the Excavation of Sardis, 1926*).

mankind its first real coinage and whose last king, Croesus, achieved fame as a monarch of legendary wealth. Assyria itself, together with the northern and eastern provinces of its former empire, became subject to the Medes. The southern and western provinces fell to the Chaldeans who established the New Babylonian Empire. Fabled Babylon was rebuilt with unprecedented splendor in glazed, colored tiles decorated with fantastic animals. This was the age of Nebuchadnezzar and the Hebrew Babylonian Captivity. It was also the age of the hanging gardens and the climax of Mesopotamian astrology. In their efforts to foretell the future and discern the wills of the gods, Chaldean wise men made painstaking observations of the stars and planets from observatories atop the towers of their fascinating city. This last brief Babylonian renaissance came to an end when the city fell to the Persians in 539.

**The Persian Empire: 539 to 330 B.C.** | The Persians, like the Medes to whom they were closely related, were an Indo-European people who had settled on the Iranian plateau. Their traditional subordination to the Medes was reversed in 549 B.C. when the Persian leader, Cyrus the Great, seized the Medean crown and thenceforth ruled both peoples. During the subsequent decade Cyrus conducted an astonishing series of military campaigns which won him a wide empire stretching from India through Mesopotamia, Lydia, and Syria-Palestine, and earned him the greatest military reputation in the history of the ancient Near East. With the conquest and absorption of Egypt shortly after Cyrus' death, the Persians unified the entire Near East into a single empire.

The Persian Empire represents the synthesis of Near Eastern political and cultural traditions under a single government that achieved stability not through military terror but through toleration. The Jews returned to their homeland and rebuilt their temple; all the peoples of the Empire were allowed a generous degree of religious and cultural autonomy. The imperial political structure was brought to its fullest development under Darius the Great (521–486 B.C.). It consisted of an absolute hereditary monarchy assisted by a central council of nobles and represented in the imperial provinces by local governors called satraps. Although the various provinces were permitted to retain many of their individual customs, the monarchy kept close watch over them through a network of imperial inspectors who saw to it that the satraps remained both honest and loyal. Commerce was stimulated by an extensive network of roads and by the introduction of imperial coinage in the Lydian tradition. The efficient Persian postal organization was commended in these familiar words: "Neither snow nor rain nor heat nor gloom of night stays these couriers from the swift completion of their appointed rounds."

The culture of the Persian Empire is a summing up rather than a new departure. In most respects it is a development of age-old Mesopotamian concepts, although the use of tall stone columns gives Persian architecture a delicate elegance all its own. The Persian King of Kings, for all his elaborate imperial pomp, refrained from claiming divinity and was satisfied merely to stress his divine appointment.

It is in the religious sphere that the Persians showed their greatest originality. They, no less than the Jews, made a sharp break with Near Eastern religious tradition. The almost legendary Persian prophet Zoroaster (or Zarathustra) proclaimed a highly intellectualized doctrine of ethical monotheism centering on the god Ahura Mazda (which means "the wise

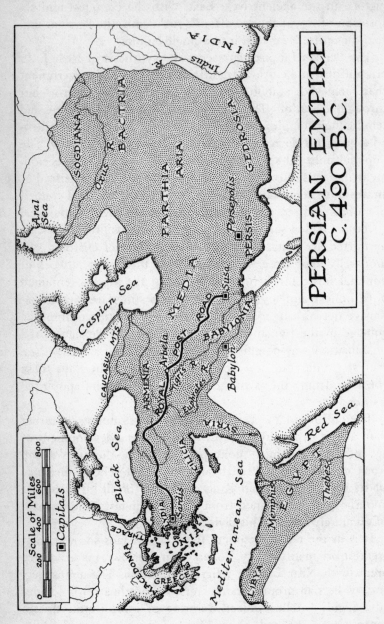

Persian Empire, 490 B.C.

lord"). In the centuries after Zoroaster's death, the traditional Persian priesthood, the Magi, appropriated the doctrine and gradually altered it, incorporating older Iranian gods into the system as subordinate deities and elevating the evil god Ahriman to a position almost equal to that of Ahura Mazda himself. Accordingly, Zoroastrianism evolved into an intensely dualistic faith that stressed the universal struggle between good and evil. Ahura Mazda became the god of light, goodness, mind, and spirit; Ahriman represented darkness, evil, and matter. The material world and the human body came to be viewed as evil; the spiritual world and the human soul as good. Zoroastrianism, alone among ancient Near Eastern religions, transcended both the state and the people that gave it birth and became a universal faith. It remained dominant in Iran and Mesopotamia until the Islamic conquests of the seventh century A.D. and exerted a powerful influence on Jewish, Hellenistic, Roman, and medieval religious thought.

The last century of Persian rule saw a failure of imperial leadership. The earlier policy of toleration gave way to repression, and political efficiency was replaced by corruption and civil strife. The consequent loss of confidence and alienation of subject peoples set the stage for the spectacular victories of Alexander the Great* that destroyed the Persian Empire in 330 B.C. and lowered the curtain on the age-long drama of the ancient Near East.

Although Near Eastern civilization collapsed politically in 330 it survived in spirit, influencing not only Alexander the Great himself but also the post-Alexandrian Hellenistic world, which witnessed a significant interplay of Greek and Oriental cultures. From the beginning Greece was profoundly indebted to the Near East which was the source of her alphabet, much of her mythology and architecture, and even the beginnings of her technology and science. The Greeks developed this intellectual and cultural legacy in ways unimagined by their predecessors. One Greek writer emphasized

*See below, Chapter 10.

Palace at Persepolis (Darius the Great). (*E. F. Schmidt, Persepolis I, 01P68, Pl. 50, Oriental Institute, University of Chicago.*)

the point with charming immodesty when he said, "Whatever the Greeks take over from foreigners, they transform it by making it something finer." Yet behind Greece and Rome lies the rich experience of the ancient Near East without which these later civilizations would be inconceivable.

| Approximate Dates B.C. | Mesopotamia | Egypt | Israel | Near East in General |
|---|---|---|---|---|
| 4000 | Formation of city-states (c.4000–2800) | | | |
| 3000 | | First Dynasties (3100–2700) | | |
| 2500 | Akkadian Empire Dynasty of Sargon (2370–2230) | Old Kingdom (2700–2200) | | |
| 2250 | | 1st Inter. Per. (2200–2050) | | |
| 2000 | | Middle Kingdom (2050–1800) | | |
| 1900 | | | | |
| 1800 | Babylonian Empire: Hammurabi's Dynasty (1790–1595) | 2nd Inter. Per. (1800–1550) | | |
| 1700 | | Hyksos (1730–1570) | | 1st Indo-European invasions (1750–1550) |
| 1600 | Political and cultural breakdown (1595–745) | | Bondage in Egypt (?1600–1350) | |
| 1500 | | New Kingdom (1550–1150) | | |
| 1400 | | Empire (1480–1165) | | |
| 1300 | | Akhnaton (1379–1361) | Moses and Sinai Period (?1350–1310) | Hittites flourish (1700?–1200) |

| Date | | | | |
|---|---|---|---|---|
| 1200 | | | | 2nd Indo-European invasions: Beginning of Iron Age (1200-900) |
| 1100 | | Post-Empire period (1150ff.) | Era of Judges (1300?-1020) | |
| 1000 | | | United Kingdom (1020-925) | |
| 900 | | | Political split: Israel and Judah (925-722) | |
| 800 | | | | |
| 700 | Assyrian Empire (745-612) | Temporary Assyrian Conquest (671) | Israel falls to Assyrians (722) | Assyrian Empire (745-612) |
| 600 | New Babylonian Empire (Chaldeans) (612-539) | Persian Conquest (525) | Judah falls: Babylonian captivity (586-539) | Lydians (fl. 683-546) Medes (fl. 612-549) Chaldeans (fl. 612-539) |
| 500 | Persian Empire (539-330) | | Return to Palestine (539 ff.) | Persian Empire (539-330) |
| 400 | | | | |
| 300 | Conquest by Alexander (330) | Conquest by Alexander (332) | | Conquest by Alexander (332-330) |

# PART ONE

# Suggested Readings

The asterisk indicates a paperback edition.

## General Works

Among several excellent textbooks on Ancient History are Chester G. Starr, *A History of the Ancient World* (Oxford), Tom B. Jones, *Ancient Civilization* (Rand McNally), Thomas W. Africa, *The Ancient World* (*Houghton Mifflin), and Richard J. Burke, *The Ancient World* (*McGraw-Hill). Also highly recommended is Tom B. Jones, *Paths to the Ancient Past* (*Free Press) and *From the Tigris to the Tiber: An Introduction to Ancient History* (*Dorsey). On a simpler level, see Chester G. Starr, *Early Man* (*Oxford).

## Mesopotamia

Sabatino Moscati, *The Face of the Ancient Orient* (*Anchor). The best single survey of ancient Near Eastern history and culture from Sumer to Persia; contains extensive quotations from the sources.

Henri Frankfort, *The Birth of Civilization in the Near East* (*Anchor). A splendid analysis of the genesis of civilization followed by illuminating discussions of early Mesopotamia and Egypt.

Henri Frankfort, ed., *Before Philosophy* (*Penguin). A brilliant, provocative series of interpretive essays on the mind of the ancient Near East.

S. N. Kramer, *History Begins at Sumer* (*Anchor). Lucid and scholarly.

Tom B. Jones, *The Sumerian Problem* (*Wiley). A well-written up-to-date essay, illuminated by excerpts from the scholarly literature, exploring the origins and contributions of the Sumerians.

*The Epic of Gilgamesh*, tr. by N. K. Sanders (*Penguin).

Seton Lloyd, *Foundations in the Dust* (*Penguin). An excellent discussion of Mesopotamian archaeology.

## Egypt

John A. Wilson, *The Culture of Ancient Egypt* (*Phoenix). The best modern introduction to Egypt, brilliant and sometimes daring in its conclusions.

J. H. Breasted, *A History of Egypt* (2nd ed., London). A durable work by the great pioneer Egyptologist.

A. Mekhitarian, *Egyptian Painting* (Skira). Gorgeously illustrated.

Christine Price, *Made in Ancient Egypt* (Dutton). On Egyptian art.


## The Diffusion of Near Eastern Civilization

O. R. Gurney, *The Hittites* (*Penguin). The authoritative survey.

H. M. Orlinsky, *Ancient Israel* (*Cornell). A brief, thoughtful summary.

A. T. Olmstead, *History of the Persian Empire* (*Phoenix). A very thorough work.

W. R. Smith, *Religion of the Semites* (*Meridian). A distinguished scholarly study.

Stanley Cook, *An Introduction to the Bible* (*Penguin). Illuminating and concise.

James B. Pritchard, ed., *The Ancient Near East* (Princeton). Near Eastern sources in translation together with a splendid group of photographs.

G. Roux, *Ancient Iraq* (*Penguin). Lucid and scholarly.

D. Harden, *The Phoenicians* (*Praeger). A readable history of Phoenician origins, overseas expansion and social history.

S. H. Hooke, *Middle Eastern Mythology* (*Penguin). A brief but comprehensive survey covering the Mesopotamians, Egyptians, Hittites, Hebrews, and early Christians.

B. H. Warmington, *Carthage* (*Penguin). A good account of Carthoginian history and civilization which describes Carthage's position in the ancient Mediterranean world.

Mary Ellen Chase, *Life and Language in the Old Testament* (*Norton). Provides a broad view of the Hebrew contribution to civilization.

# PART TWO

# GREECE

# 5

---

# Crete,
# Mycenae,
# and the Dark Age

**The New World Of The Ancient Aegean** | A century ago the
Homeric epics and the Trojan War were seen merely as inspired fancy. The picture that emerges from Homer's poems
of a highly-developed civilization in the Peloponnesus, dominated by King Agamemnon of Mycenae, was thought to be a
folk myth and nothing more. But during the 1870s and
1880s Heinrich Schliemann, a retired businessman and amateur archaeologist, confounded the scholarly world by exca-
vating Troy, Mycenae, and other Homeric sites, thereby giving reality to a supposedly imaginary civilization that had
flourished some eight centuries prior to the golden age of
Athens. Early in the present century Sir Arthur Evans exca-
vated at Cnossus on the island of Crete and found evidence of
a civilization resembling that of Mycenae on the Greek mainland, but even older and more splendid. In 1952 Michael
Ventris deciphered the *Linear B* script used at Cnossus and
several mainland sites. The work of Schliemann, Evans,
Ventris, and other students of early Aegean culture has literally opened a new world to us, but the study of this first

European civilization remains intensely fluid and exciting, with old theories constantly being upset by new discoveries.

**Minoan Civilization** | The civilization of ancient Crete has been called "Minoan" after the half-legendary King Minos of Cnossus.* It derived its technological and artistic skills from Mesopotamia, Egypt, and western Asia Minor but developed them in highly original ways. As early as the third millennium the Minoans were engaged in a vigorous trade with the Near East. Shortly after 2000 B.C. the great Minoan palaces were built. During the next six centuries these palaces were destroyed time and again by earthquakes but always rebuilt on a grander scale than before. The "palace period," between about 2000 and 1400 B.C., marks the apex of Minoan Civilization. The greatest monument of the age was the Palace of Cnossus, a magnificent rambling structure of several stories surrounding a central court. The palace contained storage rooms where tall jars of olive oil and wine were kept, a remarkable plumbing system which made possible flush toilets and baths in the beautifully decorated royal apartments, and a pillared throne room of great splendor. Minoan Crete had several smaller palaces as well as numerous luxurious private townhouses and country mansions. Surprisingly, the palaces and towns of the Minoan golden age had no appreciable fortifications. One can only conclude that the whole island was united under the kings at Cnossus and that the Minoan fleet provided sufficient protection against enemies from without.

The Minoans owed their success to their isolation and their ships. Isolation gave Crete a feeling of security, optimism, and light-heartedness reminiscent of early Egypt, but the lure of the sea resulted in a cultural dynamism that was distinctly un-Egyptian. Long before the Phoenicians ventured into the Mediterranean, Minoan seafarers were trading with Asia Minor, Syria, North Africa, the Aegean Islands, and even

---

*The name "Minos" is suspiciously similar to the names of other legendary founder-kings: Menes of Egypt, Mannus of Germany, Manu of India, and so on.

Spain. They imported tin and copper for the superb Minoan bronze ware that in turn became a chief item of export along with delicate polychrome pottery fashioned by Minoan craftsmen with consummate skill and taste. Minoan art is light and flowing; plants, animals, and marine life are portrayed with arresting naturalism. The artists produced no monumental works of sculpture but excelled at making tiny, exquisite statuettes. The Minoan style is characterized by elegance and grace rather than grandeur.

Minoan agriculture was devoted chiefly to the production of grain, wine, and olive oil—the so-called Mediterranean triad —which were also to be the chief agricultural commodities of classical Greece. The Minoan economy was exceptionally prosperous during the golden age of Crete, enabling the aristocracy to live luxuriously. Women enjoyed a relatively high status in society and are depicted in the statuettes and frescoes of the age dressed elaborately in hooped skirts with wasp waists, tight-fitting bodices that left the breasts exposed, and marvelously complex hairdos. A French archaeologist was so charmed by a fresco of one of these elegant Minoan women that he named her *La Petite Parisienne.*

The lively spirit of the Minoans is nowhere better illustrated than in their love of games. Minoan art has left us scenes of boxing matches, acrobatics, and bull-leaping. The latter, which probably had a religious significance, involved both male and female athletes grasping a bull by the horns and leaping over his body. A group of curious scholars went to the length of asking an American cowboy how this might have been done, and were told flatly that it could not be done at all. Yet bull-leaping scenes abound in Minoan art, and we can only conclude that somehow it *was* done—perhaps through the joint efforts of superbly trained athletes and an unusually obliging bull.

Minoan religion emphasized the worship of a female deity —the Earth Mother. This goddess of fertility was widely known in the Near East. We have encountered her in Sumer under the name of Inanna; she was known to the Babylonians

Hall of palace of Minos at Cnossus (*Marburg—Art Reference Bureau*).

as Ishtar, to the Egyptians as Isis, and she would later be worshipped in classical Greece as Demeter. She is depicted by Minoan sculptors in typical court dress with hoop skirt and bare breasts, sometimes with snakes in her hands. Like the later Greeks, the Minoans put little emphasis on priesthoods. Indeed, there are no Minoan temples whatever; the gods were worshipped in the palaces, at sanctuaries in private homes, and at outdoor shrines. However important religion may have been to the individual Minoan, the formal religious organization of their society was inconspicuous to a degree unknown in the ancient Near East.

**The Mycenaean Greeks** | Sometime after 2000 B.C. the first Greek-speaking peoples arrived in southern Greece. Their coming is associated with the first great Indo-European irruption into southern Europe and the Near East. From about 1580 onward the Greek settlements increasingly came under the cultural influence of Minoan civilization, although they seem to have retained their political independence. Fortress

Bull-leaping; fresco Palace at Cnossus (*Alison Frantz, Athens—Art Reference Bureau*).

cities such as Mycenae, Tiryns, and Pylos in the Peloponnesus dominated the surrounding country, and in time all the princes of southern Greece recognized the supremacy of the warrior kings of Mycenae.

These early Greeks were divided into tribes, which were then subdivided into clans. Each clan consisted of a number of related families that had their own distinctive cult and held their lands and wealth in common. The Mycenaean Greeks learned much from the Minoans; their culture differed from that of Crete chiefly in its emphasis on weapons and fortifications. They adapted the Minoan script (Linear A) to their own different language. The result was Linear B, which used a Minoan syllabary to express Greek words. Their art, architecture, and customs were all strongly influenced by the Minoans; they even took up bull-leaping, and their women began adopting Minoan dress, hairdos, and cosmetics. (The painted face has traditionally been a mark of primitivism in men; of sophistication in women.)

Before long Mycenaean sailors were challenging the Cretan

Earth Goddess, about 1700 B.C. [*Alison Frantz, Athens—Art Reference Bureau (Museum Heraklion)*].

supremacy in the Aegean. In about 1475 a band of Greeks seems to have come to power in Cnossus itself, for thereafter the Cnossan records were kept in the Greek Linear B (which is found nowhere else on Crete). In about 1400 Minoan civilization was shaken severely when a devastating invasion of the island, probably by other Mycenaean Greeks, left the towns, villas, and palaces in ruins. The great palaces were never rebuilt on their previous scale, although there is evidence that Cnossus was inhabited for several generations thereafter.

With the disintegration of the Minoan state, the Mycenaean Greeks became the masters of the eastern Mediterranean. Between about 1400 and 1200 they grew rich on their commerce and flourished exceedingly. It is at the end of this period, perhaps around 1200, that King Agamemnon of Mycenae led the Greeks against Troy. But even at the time of the Trojan War the political stability of Mycenaean Greece was being disturbed by the initial southward migrations of the Dorian Greeks and related tribes that were largely untouched by the civilizing effects of Minoan-Mycenaean culture. In about 1120 B.C. the invasions of the Peloponnesus began in earnest. The Linear B tablets found in Mycenaean cities of this era disclose frantic but vain preparations for defense. One after another, the Mycenaean cities were sacked and burned, and the civilization that had begun in Crete and later spread to the mainland came to an end at last.

**The Greek Dark Age: About 1120 to 800** | The invasions of Mycenaean Greece were associated with the second wave of Indo-European migrations between about 1200 and 900. The destruction of Mycenaean culture was approximately concurrent with the collapse of the Hittite state and the end of the Egyptian Empire. The far-flung maritime activities of the Phoenicians in the following epoch were made possible by the disruption of Mycenaean commerce. Between Mycenaean and classical Greece lies a gap of several centuries known as the "dark age" of Hellenic history. The Greeks lapsed into illiteracy, and when they began to write once again it was not in the old Minoan syllabary but in an alphabet adapted from

AEGEAN
CIVILIZATION
C.1500 B.C.

Troy

ASIA
MINOR

*Aegean Sea*

*SEA ROUTE*

Orchomenos

Mycenae
Tiryns

*Ionian Sea*

*SEA ROUTE*

RHODES

■ Capitals
0  20  40  60  80  100 Miles

Cnossus
CRETE
*SEA ROUTE*
Hagia Triada
Phaestus

Aegean civilization 1500 B.C.

the Phoenicians. The Mycenaean Greeks were violently displaced by the invasions. Most of the Peloponnesus eventually fell to the new Dorian Greeks, and in time the leadership of that area, once exercised by Mycenae, passed to the Dorian city of Sparta. Athens, as yet an unimportant town, held out against the invaders and became a haven for refugees. A group of Mycenaean Greeks known as Ionians fled across the Aegean and settled along the western coast of Asia Minor and on the islands offshore. Thenceforth, that region was known as Ionia and became an integral part of Greek civilization.* Throughout most of dark-age Greece, political conditions were chaotic and sovereignty descended to the level of the village and the clan.

*See the map on p. 77.

**Homer** | With the appearance of the Homeric epics in eighth century Ionia the darkness began to lift. Both the *Iliad* and the *Odyssey* are the products of a long oral tradition carried on by the minstrels of Mycenaean and post-Mycenaean times who recited their songs of heroic deeds at the banquets of the nobility. Whether the epics in their final form were the work of one man or several is in dispute. A number of scholars doubt that the *Iliad* and the *Odyssey* could have had a common author. Someone has suggested facetiously that the epics should not be associated with Homer at all but with an entirely different person of the same name.

Both epics are filled with vivid accounts of battle and adventure, but at heart both are concerned with ultimate problems of human life. The *Iliad*, for example, depicts the tragic consequences of the quarrel between two sensitive and passionate Greek leaders, Agamemnon and Achilles, toward the end of the Trojan War:

> Divine Muse, sing of the ruinous wrath of Achilles, Peleus' son, which brought ten thousand sorrows to the Greeks, sent the souls of many brave heroes down to the world of the dead, and left their bodies to be eaten by dogs and birds: and the will of Zeus was fulfilled. Begin where they first quarrelled, Agamemnon the King of Men, and great Achilles.*

Despite Homer's allusion to the will of Zeus, his characters are by no means puppets of the gods, even though divine intervention occurs repeatedly in his narrative. Rather they are intensely—sometimes violently—human, and they are doomed to suffer the consequences of their own deeds. In this respect, as in many others, Homer foreshadows the great Greek tragic dramatists of the fifth century B.C.

Achilles' dazzling career with its harvest of ten thousand sorrows prefigures the career of Greece itself. The gods were said to have offered Achilles the alternatives of a long but mediocre life or glory and an early death. His choice symbolizes the tragic, meteoric course of Hellenic history.

Homer was the first literate European poet and he has

*Translated by H. D. F. Kitto in *The Greeks* (rev. ed., Penguin, 1957), p. 45.

never been surpassed. The *Iliad* and the *Odyssey* were the Old and New Testament of ancient Greece, studied by every Greek schoolboy and cherished by Greek writers and artists as an inexhaustible source of inspiration. The epics were typically Greek in their rigorous and economical organization around a single great theme, their lucidity, their moments of tenderness that never slip into sentimentality—in short, their brilliantly successful synthesis of heart and mind.

**The Homeric Gods** | The gods of Mt. Olympus, who play such a significant role in the Homeric poems, had a great variety of individual backgrounds. Poseidon, the sea god, was Minoan; Zeus, the hurler of thunderbolts and ruler of Olympus, was a Dorian god; Aphrodite, the goddess of love, was an astral deity from Babylonia; Apollo and a number of others were local deities long before they entered the divine assemblage of Olympus. By Homer's time these diverse gods had been arranged into a hierarchy of related deities common to all Greeks. The Olympic gods were anthropomorphic; that is, they were human in form and personality, capable of rage, lust, jealousy, and all the other traits of the warrior-hero. But they also possessed immortality and various other superhuman attributes. The universality of the Olympic cult served as an important unifying force that compensated in part for the localism that always characterized Greek politics. Yet each clan and each district also honored its own special gods, many of whom, like Athena the patron goddess of Athens, were represented in the Olympic pantheon. The worship of these local gods was associated with feelings of family devotion or regional and civic pride. The gods were concerned chiefly with the well-being of social groups rather than the prosperity or salvation of the individual, and their worship was therefore almost indistinguishable from patriotism.

Among the lower classes ancient fertility deities remained immensely popular. Demeter, the goddess of grain, and Dionysus, the god of wine, were almost ignored in the Homeric epics but seem to have been far more important to the Greek peasantry than were the proud, aristocratic deities of Olympus. Eleusis, a small town near Athens, became the chief religious center for the worship of Demeter, and the rites celebrated there, the Eleusinian Mysteries, dramatized the ancient myth of death and resurrection. The worship of Dionysus was characterized by wild orgies during which female worshippers would dance and scream through the night. (In time these rites became more sedate and respectable.) Both Demeter and Dionysus offered their followers the hope of personal salvation and immortality that was absent from the Olympic religion. At the bottom of the social order animism persisted in all its bewildering and exotic forms. The world of the Greek peasant, like that of his Near-Eastern contemporaries, was literally crawling with gods.

# 6

## The Rise of
## Classical Greece

**The Polis** | By Homer's time, Greek culture was developing throughout the area around the Aegean Sea—in Ionia along the coast of Asia Minor, on the Aegean islands, in Athens and its surrounding district of Attica, in the Peloponnesus, and in other regions of mainland Greece.* But the Greek peoples did not coalesce into a single pan-Hellenic state. Political unity was discouraged by the roughness of the Ionian Coast, the obvious insularity of the islands, and the mountains and inlets that divided the Greek peninsula itself into a number of semi-isolated districts. The existence of the myriad city-states of ancient Greece cannot, however, be explained entirely by the environment. There are numerous examples of small independent states separated by no geographical barriers whatever —of several autonomous districts, for example, on a single island. Perhaps the Greeks lived in city-states simply as a matter of choice. Whatever the reason, classical Greek culture without the independent city-state is inconceivable.

*See the map on p. 96.

We have used the term "city-state" to describe what the Greeks knew as the "polis." Actually, "polis" is untranslatable, and "city-state" fails to convey its full meaning. In classical times the word was packed with emotional and intellectual content. Each polis had its own distinctive customs and its own gods and was an object of intense religious-patriotic devotion. More than a mere region, it was a community of citizens—the inhabitants of both town and surrounding district who enjoyed political rights and played a role in government. Words such as "political," "politics," and "polity" come from the Greek "polis"; to the Greeks, politics without the polis would be impossible. Aristotle is often quoted as saying that man is a political animal; what he really said was that man was a creature who belonged in a polis. In a vast empire like that of Persia, so the Greeks believed, slaves could live— barbarians could live—but not free and civilized people. The polis was the Greeks' answer to the perennial conflict between the individual and the state, and perhaps no other human institution has succeeded in reconciling these two concepts so satisfactorily. The Greek expressed his intense individualism *through* the polis, not in spite of it. The polis was sufficiently small that its members could behave as individuals rather than mass men; the chief political virtue was participation, not obedience. Accordingly, the polis became the vessel of Greek creativity and the matrix of the Greek spirit. A unified pan-Hellenic state might perhaps have eliminated the intercity warfare that was endemic in classical Greece. It might have brought peace, stability, and power, but at the sacrifice of the very institution that made classical Greece what it was.

Still, the system of independent warring poleis* was a remarkably inefficient basis for Greek political organization. The poleis were able to evolve and flourish only because they developed in a political vacuum. The Minoans were only a memory, and Macedonian and Roman imperialism lay in the

---

*"Poleis" is the plural of "polis."

future. During the formative period of the polis system in
the ninth, eighth, and seventh centuries, the Assyrians were
concerned primarily with maintaining their land empire and
the seafaring Phoenicians were not a dangerous military
power. The chief threat to the Greek of the dark age was the
violence of his own people. As a matter of security the inhabitants of a small district would often erect a citadel on some
central hill that they called an acropolis (high town). The
acropolis was the natural assembly place of the district in
time of war and its chief religious center. As local commerce
developed, an agora or market place usually arose at the foot
of the acropolis, and many of the farmers whose fields were
nearby built houses around the market, for reasons of socia-
bility and defense.

**The Social Orders** | At about the time that the polis was
emerging, descendants of the original tribal elders were evolving into a hereditary aristocracy. An occasional polis might
be ruled by a king (*basileus*), but, generally speaking, monarchy was diminishing; often it was reduced to a ceremonial
office. By about 700 B.C. or shortly thereafter most Greek
kings had been overthrown or shorn of all but their religious
functions, leaving the aristocracy in full control. The aristocrats had meanwhile appropriated to themselves the lion's
share of the lands that the clan members had formerly held
in common. Slowly the polis was replacing the clan as the object of primary allegiance and the focus of political activity,
but the aristocracy rode out the waves of change, growing in
wealth and power.

Below the aristocracy was a class of small farmers who had
managed to acquire fragments of the old clan common lands
or who had developed new farms on virgin soil. These Greek
yeomen had no genuine voice in political affairs and their
economic situation was always hazardous. The Greek soil is
the most barren in Europe, and while the large scale cultiva-
tion of vine and olive usually brought a profit to the aristo-
crat, the small farmer tended to sink gradually into debt. His

deplorable condition was portrayed vividly by the eighth-century poet Hesiod, a peasant himself, who wrote in a powerful, down-to-earth style. In his *Works and Days* Hesiod describes a world that had declined from a primitive golden age to the present "age of iron," characterized by a corrupt nobility and a downtrodden peasantry. For the common farmer, life was "bad in winter, cruel in summer—never good." Yet Hesiod insists that righteousness will triumph in the end. In the meantime the peasant must work all the harder: "In the sweat of your face shall you eat bread." Out of an age in which the peasant's lot seemed hopeless indeed, Hesiod proclaimed his faith in the ultimate victory of social justice and the dignity of toil.

**Colonization: 750 To 550 B.C.** | Even as Hesiod was writing his *Works and Days,* a movement was beginning that would bring a degree of relief to the small farmer and the still lower classes of the landless and dispossessed. By 750 B.C. the Greeks had once again taken to the sea—as pirates in search of booty or as merchants in search of copper and iron (rare in Greece) and the profits of trade. In this adventurous age a single crew of Greek seamen might raid and plunder one port and sell the loot as peaceful merchants in the next. During the course of their voyaging they found many fertile districts ripe for colonization, and during the two centuries between about 750 and 550 B.C. a vast movement of colonial expansion occurred that was to transform not only Greece itself but the whole Mediterranean world. Most of the more important Greek poleis sent bands of colonists across the seas to found new communities on distant shores, and in time some of these colonies sent out colonists of their own to establish still more settlements. The typical colonial polis, although bound to its mother city by ties of kinship, sentiment, and commerce and a common patriotic cult, was politically independent. We cannot speak of colonial empires in this period; even the word "colony" is a little misleading.

The motives behind the colonial movement are to be

found in the economic and social troubles afflicting the Greek homeland. Colonization meant new opportunities for the landless freeman and the struggling peasant. It provided the aristocracy with a useful safety valve against the revolutionary pressures of rising population and accumulating discontent. And there were always a few disaffected aristocrats to lead the enterprise. In the stark environment of the pioneer colony hard work was much more likely to bring its reward than in the Greece of Hesiod. Here were all the opportunities for rapid social and economic advancement commonly associated with a frontier society.

Accordingly, in the course of two centuries or so, the Greek polis spread from the Aegean region far and wide along the coasts of the Mediterranean and the Black Sea. The great Ionian polis of Miletus alone founded some eighty colonies. So many Greek settlements were established in southern Italy and Sicily that the whole area became known as *Magna Graecia*—Great Greece. The small colonial polis of Byzantium, dominating the trade route between the Black Sea and the Mediterranean, became, a millennium later, the capital of the East Roman Empire (under the name of Constantinople) and remained throughout the Middle Ages one of the greatest cities in the world. The Greek colony of Neopolis (New Polis) in southern Italy became the modern Napoli or Naples; Nikaia on the Riviera became the modern Nice; Massilia became Marseilles; Syracuse in Sicily remains to this day one of the island's chief cities. Through the poleis of *Magna Graecia* Greek culture and the Greek alphabet were transmitted to the Romans, but this was merely one important episode in a process that saw the diffusion of Greek civilization all along the shores of Southern Europe, North Africa, and Western Asia.

The colonial experience was profoundly significant in the evolution of the Greek way of life. The flourishing commerce that developed between the far-flung Hellenic settlements brought renewed prosperity to Greece itself. The homeland became an important source of wine, olive oil, and manufac-

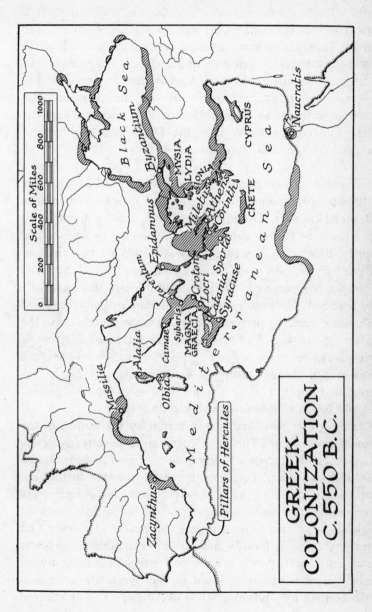

Greek colonization, 550 B.C.

tured goods for the colonies. The needs of the new settlements stimulated the growth of industrial and commercial
classes: smiths and potters, stevedores and sailors, transformed many poleis from quiet agrarian communities into bustling
mercantile centers. A new elite of merchants and manufacturers began to rival the old landed aristocrats in wealth and to
challenge their traditional monopoly of political power. During the seventh and sixth centuries many of these wealthy up-
starts elbowed their way into the councils of government
alongside the old noble families.

**The Tyrants** | The century from about 650 to 550 was an age
of fundamental economic and political change and intensified social conflict. The introduction of coinage from Lydia
was a boon to the mercantile elite but tended to sharpen and
amplify differences in wealth. It was in this age that the Ionian poet Pythermus wrote the golden line that alone of all
his works has survived: "There's nothing else that matters—
only money." The ever-increasing abundance of metal enabled
the middle class to purchase the heavy armor necessary in the
warfare of the day. And as a result, the mounted aristocratic
army of earlier times began to give way in the early seventh
century to a citizens' army of well-drilled, mailed infantry-
men called hoplites. Before long, the classes who fought for
the polis began to demand a voice in its affairs.

Class conflict was further aggravated by the waning of the
colonial movement. The best colonial sites were gradually
occupied, and the rise of new powers like Carthage in the
west and Lydia and Persia in the east prevented further expansion. As the safety valve slowly closed, the old pressures
of economic and social discontent asserted themselves with
renewed fury. One after another the poleis of Greece and
Ionia were torn by bloody civil strife as the middle and lower
classes rose against the wealthy and privileged. In many instances these conflicts resulted in the overthrow of aristocratic control by "tyrants" who, like many of their modern
counterparts, claimed to govern in the interests of the common people.

To the Greeks a tyrant was not necessarily an evil man but simply a ruler who rose to power without hereditary or legal claim. Typically, the tyrants did not smash the machinery of government but merely controlled it. They were new men, attuned to the currents of their age, who used the new coined money to hire armies of mercenaries and manipulated social discontent to their own advantage. Since they owed their power to the masses they sought to retain mass support by canceling or scaling down debts, sponsoring impressive public works projects, redistributing the lands of aristocrats, and reforming taxation. But in most Greek communities tyranny proved ephemeral. Some tyrants were overthrown by the older privileged classes; others, by the middle and lower classes who, as they became increasingly self-confident, sought to assume direct control of political affairs. By the opening of the fifth century the Greek political structure displayed every imaginable configuration of upper, lower, and middle class rule.

**Sparta** | Sparta and Athens, the two dominant poleis of the fifth century, stood at opposite ends of the Greek political spectrum. Neither played an important role in the colonization movement, for both adopted the alternative course of territorial expansion in their own districts. But while Athens evolved through the traditional stages of monarchy, aristocracy, tyranny, and democracy, Sparta acquired a peculiar mixed political system that discouraged commerce, cultural inventiveness and the amenities of life for the sake of iron discipline and military efficiency.

During the eighth and seventh centuries Sparta underwent the same political and social processes as other Greek states and played a vigorous role in the development of Greek culture. Yet from the beginning the Spartan spirit was singularly sober, and military concerns were central to Spartan life. The stern severity of its art and its Dorian architecture contrasted sharply with the charming elegance of Ionia and the cultural dynamism of Attica. Politically, Sparta had always been conservative. When the aristocracy rose to power, the monarchy was not abolished but merely weakened. With the rise of the commoners certain democratic features were incorporated into the Spartan constitution yet the monarchy and aristocracy endured. Sparta could adapt cautiously to new conditions but found it terribly difficult to abandon anything from its past.

Toward the end of the eighth century, when other Greek states were beginning to relieve their social unrest and land hunger by colonization, Sparta conquered the fertile neighboring district of Messenia, appropriating large portions of the conquered land for its own citizens and reducing many Messenians to slavery. These unfortunate people, described by a Spartan poet as "asses worn by loads intolerable," were Greeks themselves and were much too proud to accept their enslavement with resignation. In the late seventh century the Spartans crushed a Messenian revolt only after a desperate struggle. It now became clear that the Messenians could be held down only by strong military force and constant watchfulness. It was apparently at this point that Sparta transformed herself into a garrison state whose citizens became a standing army. Culture declined to the level of the barracks; the good life became the life of basic training.

Sparta became a tense, humorless society dedicated to the perpetuation, by force, of the status quo. Fear of Messenian rebellion grew into a collective paranoia as some 8000 Spartan citizens assumed the task of keeping 200,000 restless slaves in a state of permanent repression. Between the citizens and the slaves was a group of freemen without political rights who engaged in commercial activities (forbidden to the citizens themselves). The state slaves themselves—the helots—included not only Messenians but other Greek families as well, some of whom had been enslaved during the original Dorian conquests. The Spartan state divided its lands into numerous lots, one for each citizen, and the helots who worked these lots relieved the citizens of all economic responsibility, freeing them for a life of military training and service to the state.

**The Constitution of "Lycurgus"** | The writers of antiquity
ascribed the Spartan constitution to a legendary lawgiver
named Lycurgus, and despite its evolutionary elements it
operated with such rigorous logical consistency as to suggest
the hand of a single author. Sparta had two kings whose
powers had been greatly reduced by the sixth century. One
or the other of them served as supreme commander on every
military campaign, but at home their authority was overshadowed by that of three political bodies: (1) an aristocratic
council of elders, (2) an executive board of five *ephors* elected from the whole citizenry, and (3) an assembly of citizens
that included every Spartan male over thirty. Thus, Sparta
was technically a democracy, although a limited one. Every
citizen participated in the assembly, but citizenship was
denied to many freemen, to all women, and (of course) all
slaves. The Spartan assembly had the function of approving
or disapproving all important questions of state, but it did so
by acclamation rather than ballot and its members were not
permitted to debate the issues. Accordingly, the assembly
was by no means an arena of rough and tumble political conflict. It was characterized rather by the same dreary conformity that overhung all Spartan life.

The lives of Sparta's citizens were tended and guided by
the state from cradle to grave, always for the purpose of producing strong, courageous, highly disciplined soldiers. The
introduction of styles, luxuries, and ideas from without was
rigorously controlled. At a time when coinage was stimulating economic life elsewhere, Sparta used simple iron bars as
her medium of exchange. Spartan citizens seldom left their
homeland except on campaigns, and outsiders were discour-
aged from visiting Sparta. Infants were abandoned to die of
exposure if they were puny or malformed. At the age of
seven the Spartan boy was turned over to the state and spent
his next thirteen years in a program of education in military
skills, physical training, the endurance of hardships, and un-
questioning devotion to the polis. The typical product of this

system was patriotic, strong, and courageous, but incurious. At twenty he entered the citizen army and lived his next ten years in a barracks. He might marry, but he could visit his wife only if he was sufficiently resourceful to elude the barracks guards (this seems to have been regarded as a test of skill). At thirty he became a full-fledged citizen. He could now live at home, but he ate his meals at a public mess to which he was obliged to contribute the products of his assigned fields. The fare at these public messes was Spartan in the extreme. One visitor, after eating a typical meal, remarked, "Now I understand why the Spartans do not fear death."

The Spartan citizen had almost no individual existence; body and soul, he was dedicated to the state. If the helot's life was hard, so was the citizen's. Life in Sparta would seem to be a violent negation of Greek individualism, yet many Greeks were unashamed admirers of the Spartan regime. To them, Sparta represented the ultimate in self-denial and commitment to a logical idea. The Greeks admired the ordered life, and nowhere was life more ordered than in Sparta. To the Greek, there was a crucial difference between the helot and the Spartan citizen: the helot endured hardships because he had to; the citizen, because he *chose* to. And the Spartans always remembered that the object of their heroic efforts was the maintenance of the status quo—not aggressive imperialism. They were the best warriors in Greece, yet they employed their military advantage with restraint. To the accusation of artistic sterility a Spartan might reply that his state was artistic in the most basic sense of the word—that Sparta, with all its institutions directed uncompromisingly toward a single ideal, was itself a work of art.

**Athens** | Athens dates from the Mycenaean Age, but not until much later did it become prominent in Greek politics and culture. By about 700 B.C. the earlier monarchy had been deprived of political power by the aristocracy, and the entire district of Attica had been united into a single state whose political and commercial center was Athens itself. But the free inhabitants of Attica became Athenian citizens, not

Athenian slaves, and the district was held together by bonds
of mutual allegiance rather than military might. To be an
Attican was to be an Athenian.

The unification of Attica meant that the polis of Athens
comprised a singularly extensive area, and consequently the
Athenians suffered less severely from land hunger than many
of their neighbors. Athens therefore sent out no colonists,
yet as a town only four miles from the coast it was influenced by the revival of Greek commerce. Very slowly, new
mercantile classes were developing. Athenian political institutions were gradually modified, first to extend political power
to the lesser landed gentry, next to include the merchants
and manufacturers, and finally to accommodate the increasing demands of the common citizens.

**Solon And Pisistratus** | In the 590s a wise and moderate aris-
tocratic poet-statesman named Solon was given extraordinary
powers to reform the laws of Athens. His reforms left the
preponderance of political power in the hands of the wealthy
but nevertheless moved significantly in the direction of democracy. Solon's laws abolished enslavement for default of
debts and freed all debtors who had previously been enslaved.
More important, the lowest classes of free Athenian males
were now admitted into the popular assembly (whose powers
were yet distinctly limited), and a system of popular courts
was established whose judges were chosen by lot from among
the entire citizenry without regard to wealth. For the Athenian, selection by lot was simply a means of putting the choice
into the hands of the gods. Its consequence was to raise to
important offices men who were their own masters and owed
nothing to wealthy and influential political backers. Of
course the system also produced a predictable quota of
asses and nincompoops, but recent history attests that the
elective principle is by no means immune to that fault. On
the whole, selection by lot worked well in Athens and gradually became a characteristic feature of Athenian democracy.

Solon's laws were seen by many among the privileged

classes as dangerously radical, but the lower classes demanded still more reforms. The consequence of this continued popular unrest was the rise of tyranny in Athens. Between 561 and 527 a colorful tyrant named Pisistratus dominated the Athenian government. Twice he was expelled by angry aristocrats; twice he returned with the support of the commoners. At length he achieved the elusive goal of all despots: he died in power and in bed.

Pisistratus was the best of all possible tyrants: he sponsored a magnificent building program, patronized the arts, revolutionized agriculture by confiscating vast estates of recalcitrant noblemen and redistributing them among the small farmers, and established Athenian commercial outposts in the Dardanelles, thereby taking the first crucial steps along the road to empire. He gave Athens peace, prosperity, and a degree of social and economic harmony that it had long needed. The agrarian dilemma that had afflicted Attica for generations was effectively solved. The polis was at peace with itself at last.

**The Constitution Of Cleisthenes** | Pisistratus' two sons and successors proved incompetent and oppressive. One was assassinated; the other was driven from power by exiled nobles who returned with Spartan military support. But many of the aristocrats had grown wise in exile and were willing to accept popular rule. Under the leadership of a statesmanlike aristocrat named Cleisthenes a new and thoroughly democratic constitution was established in the closing decade of the sixth century which became the political basis of Athen's most glorious age. Cleisthenes administered the final blow to the aristocratic leaders of the old tribes and clans. Until the time of his reforms loyalty to clan and tribe had remained strong. Now Cleisthenes abolished these ancient groups, replacing them with ten new "tribes" whose membership was no longer based on kinship. Each of the ten tribes was made up of numerous small territorial districts scattered throughout Attica. Consequently, members of every class—commerical, industrial, rural, and aristocratic—were about evenly divided among the ten tribes.

Cleisthenes may also have been responsible for introducing the principle of ostracism, which provided a further safeguard against the evils of violent factionalism.* Each year the Athenians decided by vote whether or not they would ostracize one of their number. If they decided affirmatively, then any citizen might propose the name of a person whom he considered a threat to the well-being of the polis. Whichever candidate received the most votes in the Assembly was banished from Athens for ten years. He kept his citizenship and his property but was no longer in a position to interfere with the operation of the polis.

All matters of public policy were decided by the Assembly whose membership included all Athenian citizens from landless laborers to great aristocrats. As in Sparta and elsewhere in Greece, citizenship was limited to males, but in Athens it came to include every freeman of eighteen years or over. In the mid-fifth century the total Athenian citizenry has been estimated at about 50,000 men. There were also, exclusive of women and children, about 25,000 resident aliens called "metics" who were free but without political rights, and perhaps some 55,000 adult male slaves. When we speak of Athenian democracy we must always remember that a considerable group of Athenians were enslaved and that slaves and women had no voice in politics whatever. Nevertheless, citizenship was far less exclusive than in Sparta, and with respect to the citizenry itself Athens was more thoroughly democratic than any modern state. The citizens did not elect the legislators; they *were* the legislators.

For the transaction of day-to-day business, Cleisthenes provided a smaller body—a Council of Five Hundred—for which every Athenian citizen over thirty was eligible. The Council was made up of fifty men from each tribe chosen an-

*Ostracism may have been introduced into Athens at a somewhat later date. The first recorded use is in 488.

nually by lot from a list of tribal nominees. Each of these
fifty-man tribal groups served for one-tenth of a year. Their
order of rotation was determined by a crude machine which
archaeologists have recently discovered. It worked much like
our modern bubble gum machines: a stone for each of the
ten tribes was put in the machine, and each month one stone
was released, thus preventing any tribe except the last from
knowing in advance when its term would begin. Random selection pervaded the Athenian constitution. Every day a different chairman for the fifty-man panel was chosen by lot.
Most of the various magistrates and civil servants also came to
be selected by lot for limited terms and were strictly responsible to the Council of Five Hundred and the Assembly. This
was a citizens' government in every sense of the word—a government of amateurs rather than professional bureaucrats.

Neither Council nor Assembly could provide the long
range personal leadership so essential to the well-being of the
state. The Assembly was too unwieldy, the Council too cir-
cumscribed by rotation and lot. Consequently, the chief executive power in Athens came to be exercised by a group of
ten generals (*strategoi*), one from each tribe, who were elected annually by the Assembly and were eligible for indefinite
re-election. Even the most zealous democrat could scarcely
wish to see his generals chosen by lot or rotated every year.
These were offices for which special talent was essential, and
the Athenians wisely tended to choose as their *strategoi* men
from the aristocracy who had behind them a long tradition of
military and political experience. The greatest Athenian *stra-
tegos* of the fifth century, Pericles, was precisely such a man,
and his extended tenure in office illustrates the remarkable
equilibrium achieved in the golden age between aristocratic
leadership and popular sovereignty. Even Pericles was subject
to the Assembly on which he depended for support and re-
election. He could exercise his authority only by persuasion
or political manipulation—never by force.

The success of the Greek polis in achieving harmony between the individual and society was nowhere more complete

than in Athens, the scene of man's first significant encounter with democracy. The Athenian historian Thucydides expressed this achievement in words that he attributed to Pericles himself:

> . . . Our constitution is called a democracy because it is in the hands not of the few but of the many. But our laws secure equal justice for all in their private disputes, not as a matter of privilege but as a reward of merit . . . Alone of all states we regard a man who holds aloof from public life not as harmless but as useless; we deliberate in person all matters of policy, holding not that words and deeds go ill together, but that acts are foredoomed to failure when undertaken undiscussed . . . . In short, I say that Athens is the school of Hellas, and that her citizens yield to none, man for man, in independence of spirit, many-sidedness of attainment, and self-reliance in body and mind.*

*From Pericles' Funeral Oration, in Thucydides, *History of the Peloponnesian War*. I am following the translation of Sir Alfred Zimmern with slight modifications.

# 7

## The Zenith and Decline of Classical Greece

**Ionia, Lydia, and Persia** | During the sixth century, while Solon, Pisistratus, and Cleisthenes were transforming Athens into a prosperous democracy, the cultural center of the Hellenic world was Ionia. Here, on the shores of Asia Minor, the Greeks came into direct contact with the ancient Near East. The results of this contact were fruitful indeed, for the Ionian Greeks adapted Near Eastern art, architecture, literature, and learning to their own distinctive outlook. They created a brilliant, elegant culture, far more gracious and luxurious than any that existed in Greece itself. It was in this setting that Greek philosophy, science, and lyric poetry were born. Ionian poleis underwent much the same political and economic developments as those of Greece, and by the sixth century the lower classes were attempting to overthrow the control of the aristocrats. In the Ionian city of Miletus the aristocrats and commoners went to the extreme of burning one another alive.

These internal social struggles were affected drastically by the intervention of outside powers. During the 560s and 550s the coastal cities of Ionia fell one by one under the control of the Lydians, and when Lydia was conquered by Cyrus the Great in 546 they passed under Persian control. In 499 there occurred a general Ionian rebellion against Persian rule, during which the Athenians were persuaded to send twenty ships to aid their desperate kinsmen. But the Athenian aid proved insufficient and by 494 the Persians had crushed the insurrection, punctuating their victory by sacking Miletus. Ionia's gamble for independence had failed and, even more important, Darius the Great of Persia was now bent on revenge against Athens. The Persian Wars, Herodotus observes, were precipitated by the sending of twenty ships.

**The Persian Wars: To 479 B.C.** | In 490 Darius led an army across the Aegean to teach the Greeks a lesson in respect. As was so often the case, the Greeks, even in the face of this calamity, found it impossible to unite. The Spartans held aloof in the Peloponnesus, claiming that they could not send their army until the moon's phase was auspicious, and other citystates preferred to await further developments. Consequently Athens was obliged to face the Persians almost alone. At Marathon in Attica the two armies met, and the Athenian hoplites, fighting shoulder to shoulder for the preservation of their homes and their polis, won a brilliant victory. 6400 Persians fell at Marathon while only 192 Greeks lost their lives.

Marathon was not won by Athenian heroism alone. At the time of the battle the Persians were bogged down in a difficult sea landing with their cavalry still aboard ship. And the Athenians, although outnumbered, enjoyed great superiority in armament (the Persians were said to have used wicker shields). Nevertheless, the Athenian victory was a notable achievement. It won Greece an invaluable postponement of the Persian threat, and it generated in Athens a powerful sense of pride and self-confidence. The sovereign of the world's greatest empire had been defeated by a small army of free Athenian citizens. For such men as these, so it seemed, nothing was impossible. The epitaph attributed to the great

Athenian dramatist Aeschylus contains no mention of his literary achievements but only the proud statement that he had
fought at Marathon.

The buoyant optimism that filled Athens in the wake of
Marathon was tempered by the sobering thought that the Persians were likely to return in far greater numbers. Darius
spent his last years planning a devastating attack against
Greece, but when the new invasion came in 480 it was led by
Darius' successor, Xerxes. A Persian army of about 180,000
fighting men, stupendous by the standards of the age, moved
by land around the northern Aegean shore accompanied by a
powerful armada.

Xerxes had paved his way into Greece by alliances with a
number of opportunistic Greek cities such as Argos and
Thebes. In the meantime Athens had been preparing for the
onslaught under the enterprising leadership of Themistocles,
a statesman of great strategic imagination, who saw clearly
that Athens' one hope was to build a strong fleet and seize
control of the Aegean from the Persian Empire. By the time
Xerxes led his forces into Greece, Themistocles' fleet was
ready.

Sparta had by now awakened to the danger of a Persian
conquest and was equally alarmed at the possibility of
Athens winning additional prestige from another single-
handed victory. During the sixth century Sparta had aimed
her wars and diplomacy toward the establishment of a Peloponnesian League for the purpose of increasing her own security. By the end of the century nearly every state in the
Peloponnesus had joined the League including the wealthy
commercial polis of Corinth. Each League member had one
vote, but Sparta alone had the privilege of summoning and
presiding over the League's assembly and was usually able to
dominate it. Now, in the shadow of Xerxes' invasion, representatives of the Peloponnesian states met at Corinth with
delegates from Athens and a number of other poleis. Here
they agreed to form a much larger organization—a Pan-Hellenic League—to coordinate the common defense.

As Xerxes moved southward through northern Greece a
small army of Spartans and other Greeks led by the Spartan
King Leonidas placed itself across the Persian path at Thermopylae, a narrow pass between sea and mountains through
which Xerxes' host had to move before breaking into the
south. When the two armies met, the Persians found that
their immense numerical superiority was of little use on so
restricted a battlefield and that man for man they were no
match for the Greeks. But at length a Greek turncoat led a
contingent of the Persian army along a poorly defended path
through the mountains to the rear of the Greek position.
Now completely surrounded, the Greeks continued to fight
and died to the last man in defense of the field. Although the
battle of Thermopylae was a defeat for the Spartans, it was
also a symbol of their dedication and courage. The inscrip-
tion that was later placed over their graves is a model of Spartan brevity and understatement:

> Tell them the news in Sparta, passer by,
> That here, obedient to their words, we lie.*

Much delayed, Xerxes' army now moved against Athens.
The Athenians, at Themistocles' bidding, evacuated Attica
and took refuge elsewhere, some in the Peloponnesus, others
on the island of Salamis just off the Attican coast. The refugees on the island had to look on helplessly as the Persians
plundered Athens and burned the temples on the Acropolis.
But Themistocles' strategy was vindicated when the Greek
and Persian fleets fought a decisive naval engagement in the
Bay of Salamis. The Bay provided insufficient room for the
huge Persian armada to maneuver, and the lighter, faster
Greek fleet, with the new Athenian navy as its core, won an
overwhelming victory.

Persia's navy was decimated before the eyes of Xerxes who
witnessed the disaster from a rocky headland. Commanding

---

*Yet, paradoxically, the probable author of this epigram, Simonides, was not a
Spartan. Poets do not abound in a barracks state.

his army to withdraw to northern Greece for the winter, Xerxes himself departed for Asia never to return. In the following spring (479) the Persian army was routed at Plataea on the northern frontier of Attica by a Pan-Hellenic army under Spartan command. And the Greeks won a final victory over the tattered remnants of the Persian army and fleet at Cape Mycale in Ionia. Now, one after another, the Ionian cities were able to break loose from Persian control. Hellas had preserved its independence and was free to work out its own destiny.

As an ironic postscript to the momentous struggle, Themistocles, the key figure in Athens' triumph at Salamis, fell from power shortly thereafter. Exiled from Athens, he ended his days in the service of the king of Persia.

**The Athenian Empire** | To some historians the moment of truth for classical Greece was not Marathon, Salamis, or Plataea, but rather the brief period immediately afterward when the possibility of establishing the Pan-Hellenic League on a permanent basis was allowed to slip by. Yet as more recent history attests, it is easier to unite against a common foe than to maintain a wartime confederation in the absence of military necessity. Common fear is a stronger cement than common hope, and the creation of a Pan-Hellenic state from the Greek alliance of 480 to 479 was of the same order of difficulty as the creation of a World State from the United Nations of World War II. Considering the intense involvement of the typical Greek in his polis, it seems doubtful that Greek federalism was ever a genuine option.

Nevertheless, the Greek world in 479, lacking our advantage of hindsight, could not be certain that the Persian invasions were truly over. Sparta, always fearful of a helot revolt at home, withdrew from the League to concentrate on her own affairs, and Sparta's Peloponnesian confederates withdrew also. Athens, however, was unwilling to lower her guard. A large fleet had to be kept in readiness, and such a fleet could not be maintained by Athens alone. Consequently a new alliance was formed under Athenian leadership that included most of the maritime poleis on the coasts and islands of the Aegean from Attica to Ionia.

The alliance was known as the Delian League because its headquarters and treasury were on the island of Delos, an ancient Ionian religious center. Athens and a few other cities contributed ships to the Delian fleet; the remaining members contributed money. All were entitled to a voice in the affairs of the Delian League, but Athens, with its superior wealth and power, gradually assumed a dominant position.

Slowly the Delian League evolved into an Athenian Empire. In 454 the League treasury was transferred from Delos to Athens, where its funds were diverted to the welfare and adornment of Athens itself. The Athenians justified this extraordinary financial sleight of hand by the argument that their fleet remained always vigilant and ready to protect League members from Persian aggression, but their explanation was received unsympathetically in some quarters. An Ionian visiting Athens might well admire the magnificent new temples being erected on the Acropolis but his admiration would be chilled by the reflection that his own polis was contributing financially toward their construction.

Certain members attempted to withdraw from the League, both before and after the transfer of the treasury. But they quickly discovered that Athens regarded secession as illegal and was ready to enforce the continued membership of disillusioned poleis by military action. With the development of this policy in the 460s, the transformation from Delian League to Athenian Empire was complete.

The half century between Salamis and the opening of the Peloponnesian War (480–431) was the Athenian Golden Age. The empire rose and flourished, bringing Athens unimagined wealth, not merely from imperial assessments but also from the splendid commercial opportunities offered by Athenian domination of the Aegean. Athens was now the commercial capital of the Mediterranean world and the great power in Greece. Sparta and her Peloponnesian allies held aloof, yet

Athenian statesmen such as Pericles hoped that one day they too would be brought by force under Athens' sway.

**The Golden Age** | The economic and imperialistic foundations of Athens' Golden Age are interesting to us chiefly as a backdrop for the cultural explosion that has echoed through the centuries of Mediterranean and European civilizations. Through a rare and elusive conjunction of circumstances a group of some 50,000 politically conscious Athenian citizens created in the decades after Salamis a unique, many-sided culture of superb taste and unsurpassed excellence. The culture of the Golden Age was anticipated in the sixth and even earlier centuries, and the period of creativity continued, especially in the intellectual sphere, into the fourth. But the zenith of Greek culture was reached in imperial Athens during the administration of Pericles in the middle decades of the fifth century. The next two chapters will examine this achievement more closely. For now, suffice it to say that fifth century Athens has served Western Civilization as an example of what the human spirit at its best is capable of attaining.

The Athenian achievement is so glittering that one is in danger of viewing the Golden Age as an utopia. In reality the architecture and sculpture of the Acropolis, the tragic dramas, the probing philosophical speculation, were produced against a background of large-scale slavery, petty politics, commercial greed, and growing imperial arrogance. Pericles, who remained in power almost continuously from shortly after 460 to his death in 429, provided much-needed direction to democratic Athens, but he maintained the support of the commercial classes by advocating an ever-expanding empire.

Pericles' policy of extending Athenian imperialism to dominate the entire Greek world aroused the hostility of Sparta and its Peloponnesian League. Corinth, the second greatest city in the League and Athens' chief commercial rival, was especially apprehensive of Pericles' imperialism. In 431 these accumulating tensions resulted in a war between the Peloponnesian League and the Athenian Empire—a protracted, agonizing struggle that ultimately destroyed the Athenian Empire and shook the Greek political structure to its foundations. The fifth century saw the polis system at its best and at its worst: on the one hand, the culture of Periclean Athens; on the other, the Peloponnesian War.

**The Peloponnesian War** | The war ran from 431 to 404. For the most part it was a matter of a whale fighting an elephant. Athens was invincible by sea, Sparta, by land. When the Spartans marched into Attica year after year to devastate the fields, the population would withdraw behind the protection of Athens' walls and live off foodstuffs imported by the fleet. Democratic Athens and regimented Sparta represented two contrary political systems, and the disparity was intensified by the fact that each of the two tended to reproduce its own political structure in the states dependent on it. Sparta encouraged oligarchy (rule by the few) throughout the Peloponnesus while Athens was inclined to give her support to democratic factions within the cities of her empire. Yet the Peloponnesian War was not so much an ideological conflict as a simple power struggle. Athens dreamed of bringing all Hellas under her sway, and Sparta and its allies were determined to end the threat of Athenian imperialism. Athens was coming to be regarded as a tyrant among the states of her own empire, but so long as Athenian ships patrolled the Aegean, rebellion was minimized. Paradoxically, the mother of democracies was driven to ever more despotic expedients to hold her empire together.

In 430 and 429 Athens, crowded with refugees, was struck by a plague that carried off perhaps a quarter of its population including Pericles himself. The loss of this far-sighted statesman, combined with the terrible shock of the plague, led to a rapid deterioration in the quality of Athenian government. Leadership passed into the hands of extremists, and the democracy acquired many of the worst characteristics of

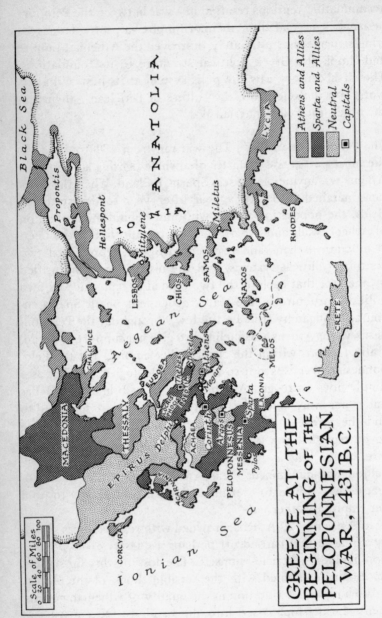

## GREECE AT THE BEGINNING OF THE PELOPONNESIAN WAR, 431 B.C.

Scale of Miles
0  20  40  60  80  100

Athens and Allies
Sparta and Allies
Neutral
□ Capitals

Black Sea

ANATOLIA

Propontis

Hellespont

IONIA

Mitylene

LESBOS

CHIOS

Miletus

SAMOS

Aegean Sea

NAXOS

LYCIA

RHODES

CHALCIDICE

MACEDONIA

THESSALY

EPIRUS

EUBOEA

Delphi

Thebes

Plataea

Athens

Megara

CORCYRA

ACARNANIA

ACHAEA

Corinth

Argos

PELOPONNESUS

MESSENIA

Pylos

Sparta

LACONIA

MELOS

CRETE

Ionian Sea

Greece, 431 B.C.

mob rule. A general who, through no fault of his own, failed to win some battle might be sent into exile. (Such was the experience of Thucydides, Athens' greatest historian). When the Athenians captured the island of Melos, an innocent neutral in the struggle, all its men were slaughtered and its women and children sold as slaves.

Pericles observed on the eve of the war that he was more afraid of Athens' mistakes than of Sparta's designs. His fear was well founded, for as the war progressed along its dreary course Athenian strategy became increasingly reckless. The better part of the Athenian fleet was lost when two ill-planned expeditions against distant Syracuse ended in complete disaster. As Athens' grip on the Aegean loosened, her subject cities began to rebel, and at length a Peloponnesian fleet, financed in part by Persian gold, destroyed what was left of Athens' navy.

In 404 Athens surrendered—her wealth lost, her spirit broken, and her empire in ruins. Long thereafter she remained the intellectual and cultural center of the Greek world—she was even able to make something of an economic and political recovery—but her years of imperial supremacy were behind her.

**The Fourth Century** | The period between the end of the Peloponnesian War in 404 and the Macedonian conquest of Greece in 338 was an age of chaos and anticlimax during which the polis system was drained of its creative force by incessant intercity warfare and a disastrous decline in social responsibility. The immediate result of Athens' surrender was Spartan hegemony over the Greek world. The victorious Spartan fleet had been built with Persian money, and Sparta paid her debt by allowing Persia to reoccupy Ionia. The Spartans were much too conservative to be successful imperialists, and although for a time they followed a policy of establishing oligarchic regimes in the poleis of Athens' former empire—indeed, in Athens herself— they quickly proved incapable of giving direction to Hellas.

In Athens and in many other states the oligarchies were soon overthrown, and Greece passed into a bewildering period of military strife and shifting hegemonies. For a brief period Thebes rose to supremacy. Athens herself began to form a new Aegean league only to be frustrated by Persian intervention. In the middle decades of the fourth century power tended to shift between Sparta, Athens, and Thebes, while the Greek colony of Syracuse dominated Sicily and southern Italy. Envoys from Persia, always well supplied with money, saw to it that no one state became too powerful. A Greece divided and decimated by incessant warfare could be no threat to the Persian Empire.

Ironically, Persia's diplomacy paved the way for an event that she had been determined at all costs to avoid: the unification of Greece. The debilitating intercity wars left Greece unprepared for the intervention of a new power on its northern frontier. Macedon was a mountain kingdom whose inhabitants, although distantly related to the Greeks, knew almost nothing of Hellenic culture. In 359 a talented opportunist named Philip became king of Macedon. He tamed and unified the Macedonian tribes, secured his northern frontiers, and then began a patient and artful campaign to bring Greece under his control.

Having spent three years of his boyhood as a hostage in Thebes, Philip of Macedon had acquired a full appreciation of both Greek culture and Greek political instability. He hired the philosopher Aristotle as tutor for his son Alexander, and he exploited the ever-increasing Greek distaste for war by bluffing and cajoling his way into the south. His conquests of Greek towns were accompanied by declarations of his peaceful intentions, and when at last Athens and Thebes resolved their ancient rivalry and joined forces against him it was much too late. At Chaeronea in 338 Philip won the decisive battle and Greece lay at his mercy.

Philip allowed the Greek states to run their own internal affairs but he organized them into a league whose policies he controlled. With the subordination of Greek freedom to the will of King Philip the classical age of Greek history came to an end. With the accession of Philip's illustrious son, Alexander the Great, two years later, a new age began which would see the spread of Greek culture throughout the Near East and the transformation of Greek life into something drastically different from what it had been before.

**The Decline Of The Polis** | Classical Greece was a product of the polis, and when the polis lost its meaning classical Greece came to an end. The essence of the polis was participation in the political and cultural life of the community. The citizen was expected to take care of his private business and at the same time attend the assembly, participate in decisions of state, serve in the administration, and fight in the army or navy whenever necessary. Statesmen such as Pericles were at once administrators, orators, and generals. The polis at its best was a community of well-rounded men—men who had many interests and capabilities—in short, amateurs.

In the sixth and early fifth centuries, when Greek life had been comparatively simple, it was possible for one man to play many roles. But as the fifth century progressed the advantages of specialization grew. Military tactics became more complex. Administrative procedures became increasingly refined. Oratory became the subject of specialized study. As the various intellectual disciplines progressed it became more and more difficult to master them. The age of the amateur gradually gave way to the age of the professional. The polis of the fourth century was filled with professional administrators, orators, scholars, bankers, sailors, and businessmen whose demanding careers left them time for little else. Citizens were becoming absorbed in their private affairs, and political life, once the very embodiment of the Greek spirit, was losing its fascination. Citizen-soldiers gave way increasingly to mercenaries, partly because civic patriotism was running dry but also because fighting was now a full-time career. The precarious equilibrium achieved in the Golden Age between competence and versatility—between individual and commu-

nity—could only be momentary, for the intense creativity of
the fifth century led inevitably to the specialization of the
fourth. It has been said that "Progress broke the Polis,"* yet
progress was a fundamental ingredient of the way of life that
the polis created.

*Kitto, *The Greeks,* p. 161.

# 8

## The Hellenic Mind

The intellectual achievement of the Greeks has been of immense importance to Western Civilization. The civilizations of the ancient Near East did significant pioneer work in mathematics, engineering and practical science; the Hebrews developed a profound ethical system based on divine revelation. But it was the Greeks who first took the step of examining man and his universe from a rational standpoint. It was they who transcended the mythical and poetic approach to cosmology and began to look at the universe as a natural rather than a supernatural phenomenon, based on discoverable principles of cause and effect rather than on divine volition. It was they who first attempted to base morality and the good life on reason rather than revelation.

Accordingly, the Greeks were the first philosophers—the first logicians—the first theoretical scientists. The Babylonians had studied the stars to prophesy; the Egyptians had mastered geometry to build tombs, and chemistry to create mummies; the Greeks had much to learn from their predecessors, but they turned their knowledge and their investigation

toward a new end: a rational understanding of man and the
universe. Their achievement has been described as "the discovery of the mind."

This is not to say that the Greeks were irreligious. Their
dramas, their civic festivals, their Olympic Games were all religious celebrations; their art and architecture were devoted
largely to honoring the gods; their generals sometimes altered
their strategy on the basis of some divine portent. But the
Greek philosophers succeeded by and large in holding their
gods at bay and untangling the natural from the supernatural.
Like the Jews, they rejected the "I-thou" relationship of man
and nature, but unlike the Jews they were not intensely involved in the worship of a single, omnipotent deity. The
Greeks had no powerful official priesthood to enforce correct
doctrine. To them, as to other ancient peoples, the cosmos
was awesome. But they possessed the open-mindedness and
the audacity to probe it with their intellects.

**Ionia: The Lyric Poets** | Open-mindedness and audacity—so
alien to the absolute monarchies of the Near East—were nourished by the free and turbulent atmosphere of the polis.
Greek rationalism was a product of Greek individualism, and
among the first manifestations of this new spirit of self-
awareness and irreverence for tradition was the development
of lyric poetry in seventh- and sixth-century Ionia.

Greek lyric poetry was a literary achievement, but its importance transcends the field of belles lettres. The works of
lyric poets such as Archilochus in the seventh century and
Sappho of Lesbos in the sixth disclose self-consciousness and
intensity of experience far exceeding anything before. At a
time when Spartan mothers were sending their sons to war
with the stern admonition, "Return with your shield—or on
it," the Ionian Archilochus was expressing a far more individ-
ualistic viewpoint:

> Some lucky Thracian has my shield,
>    For, being somewhat flurried,

> I dropped it by a wayside bush,
>   As from the field I hurried;
> Thank God, I made it clear away,
>   To blazes with the shield!
> I'll get another just as good
>   When next I take the field.

With such lines as these Archilochus ceases to be a mere name and emerges as a vivid, engaging personality. He is history's first articulate coward.

The most intensely personal of the lyric poets was Sappho, an aristocratic woman of sixth-century Lesbos, who became the directress of a school for young girls—apparently a combination finishing school and religious guild dedicated to Aphrodite, the goddess of Love. Her passionate love lyrics to her students have raised puritanical eyebrows and have given enduring meaning to the word "lesbian"; the people of antiquity saw Sappho as the Tenth Muse and the equal of Homer. Never before had human feelings been expressed with such perception and sensitivity:

> Love has unbound my limbs and set me shaking
> A monster bitter-sweet and my unmaking.*

**The Ionian Philosophers** | The same surge of individualism that produced lyric poetry gave rise to mankind's first effort to understand rationally the physical universe. So far as we know the first philosopher and theoretical scientist in human history was the sixth-century Ionian, Thales of Miletus, who set forth the proposition that water was the primal element of the universe. This hypothesis, although crude by present standards, constitutes a significant effort to impose a principle of intellectual unity on the diversity of experience. The world was to be understood as a single physical substance. Presumably solid objects were made of compressed water, air of rarefied water, and empty space of dehydrated water.

---

*Greek Literature in Translation, ed. Oates and Murphy, p. 972.

Thales' hypothesis did not commend itself to his successors, but the crucial point is that Thales had successors—that other men, following his example, would continue the effort to explain the universe through natural rather than supernatural principles. Intellectual history had taken a bold new turn.

The Ionian philosophers after Thales continued to speculate about the primal substance of the universe. One suggested that air was the basic element; another, fire. The Ionian Anaximander set forth a primitive theory of evolution and declared that men were descended from fish. But these intellectual pioneers, their originality notwithstanding, disclose a basic weakness that characterized Greek thought throughout the classical age: an all-too-human tendency to rush into sweeping generalizations on the basis of a grossly inadequate factual foundation. Beguiled by the potentialities of rational inquiry, they failed to appreciate how painfully difficult it is to arrive at sound conclusions. Consequently, the hypotheses of the Ionians are of the nature of inspired guesses. Anaximander's theory of evolution, for example, was quickly forgotten because, unlike Darwin's, it had no significant supporting data.

**The Pythagorean School** | Pythagoras (about 582–507 B.C.) represents a different intellectual trend. A native of Ionia, he migrated to southern Italy where he founded a brotherhood, half scientific, half mystical. He drew heavily from the mystery cults of Dionysus and Demeter. He was influenced especially by Orphism, a salvation cult that was becoming popular in the sixth century. The cult of Orpheus stressed guilt and atonement, a variety of ascetic practices, and an afterlife of suffering or bliss depending on the purity of one's soul. This and similar cults appealed to those who found inadequate solace in the heroic but worldly gods of Olympus. Following the basic structure of Orphic dogma, Pythagoras and his followers advocated the doctrine of transmigration of souls and the concept of a quasi-monastic communal life. Entangled in all this was their profoundly significant notion that the basic element in nature was neither water, air, nor fire, but *number*. The Pythagoreans studied the intervals between musical tones and worked out basic laws of harmony. Having demonstrated the relationship between music and mathematics, they next applied these principles to the whole universe, asserting that the cosmos obeyed the laws of harmony and, indeed, that the planets in their courses produced musical tones which combined into a cosmic rhapsody: the music of the spheres. Implicit in this bewildering mixture of insight and fancy is the pregnant concept that nature is best understood mathematically.

Their mathematical thought was clouded by a superstitious reverence for the number ten which they saw as magical. Consequently, they have inspired a great deal of numerological foolishness down to our own day. But they also played a crucial role in the development of mathematics and mathematical science. They produced the Pythagorean theorem and the multiplication table, and their notions contributed to the development of modern science in the sixteenth and seventeenth centuries. The Greeks were at their best in mathematics, for here they could reason deductively—from self-evident concepts—and their distaste for the slow, patient accumulation of data was no hindrance.

**The Fifth Century** | In the course of the fifth century a great many of the central problems that have occupied philosophers ever since were raised and explored: whether the universe is in a state of constant flux or eternally changeless; whether it is composed of one substance or many; whether or not the nature of the universe can be grasped by the reasoning mind. Democritus (fl. 440) set forth a doctrine of materialism that anticipated several of the views of modern science. He maintained that the universe consists of countless atoms in random configurations—that it has no center and no periphery but is much the same one place as another. In short, the universe is infinite and the earth is in no way unique. Like Anaximander's theory of evolution, Democritus' atomism was essentially a philosophical assertion rather than a scientific hypothesis based on empirical evidence, and since infinity was not a concept congenial to the Greek mind, atomism long remained a minority view. But in early modern times Democritus' notion of an infinite universe contributed significantly to the development of a new philosophical outlook and to the rise of modern astronomy.

It was in medicine and history rather than in cosmology that the Greeks of the fifth century were able to resist the lure of the spectacular generalization and concentrate on the humble but essential task of accumulating verified facts. In the field of medicine, Hippocrates and his followers recorded case histories with scrupulous care and avoided the facile and hasty conclusion. Their painstaking clinical studies and their rejection of supernatural causation started medicine upon its modern career.

A similar reverence for the verifiable fact was demonstrated by the Greek historians of the period. History, in the modern sense, begins with Herodotus, a man of boundless curiosity who, in the course of his extensive travels, gathered a vast accumulation of data for his brilliant and entertaining history of the Persian Wars. Herodotus made a serious effort to separate fact from fable, but he was far surpassed in this regard by Thucydides, a disgraced Athenian general who wrote his account of the Peloponnesian War with unprecedented objectivity and an acute sense of historical criticism. "Of the events of the war," writes Thucydides, ". . . I have described nothing but what I either saw myself or learned from others whom I questioned most carefully and specifically. The task was laborious, because eyewitnesses of the same events gave different accounts of them, as they remembered or were interested in the actions of one side or the other."

Thucydides' philosophy of history was radically different from that of the Hebrews. To him, history was not a product of divine planning but rather the outgrowth of political action on the part of statesmen and popular assemblies. His approach was not social or economic as is that of many modern historians, but political and psychological. His chief interest lay in the motivations underlying political action, and he subjected the political conflicts in the Greek poleis to keen and rigorous analysis. To Thucydides, the polis was a fascinating arena where diverse political views contended, and since he was inclined to view political issues as the central problems of existence, he ascribed to the polis a dominant role in the dynamics of history. Here, as elsewhere, Thucydides' thought was characteristically Greek.

**The Sophists** | In philosophy, history, and science, reason was winning its victories at the expense of the supernatural. The anthropomorphic gods of Olympus were especially susceptible to rational criticism, for few people who were acquainted with Ionian philosophy or the new traditions of scientific history and medicine could seriously believe that Zeus hurled thunderbolts or that Poseidon caused earthquakes. Some philosophical spirits came to see Zeus as a transcendent god of the universe; others rejected him altogether.

But if one doubts that Zeus tosses thunderbolts one is also likely to doubt that Athena protects Athens. And the rejection of Athena and other civic deities was bound to be subversive to the traditional spirit of the polis. Religious skepticism was gradually undermining civic patriotism, and as skepticism advanced, patriotism receded. Once again we are brought face to face with the dynamic and paradoxical nature of the Greek experience: the polis produced the inquiring mind, but in time the inquiring mind eroded the most fundamental traditions of the polis.

The arch skeptics of fifty-century Athens were the Sophists, a diverse group of professional teachers drawn from every corner of the Greek world by the wealth of the great city. Much of our information about the Sophists comes from the writings of Plato, who disliked them heartily and portrayed them as intellectual prostitutes and tricksters. In reality most of them were dedicated to the life of reason and the sound argument. Unlike the Ionian philosophers, they were chiefly interested in man rather than the cosmos. They investigated ethics, politics, history, and psychology and have been called the first social scientists. In applying reason to these areas and teaching their students to do the same, they aroused the wrath of the conservatives and doubtless encouraged an irreverent attitude toward tradition. Of course, the Greeks were not nearly so tradition-bound as other peoples of their era, but there is a limit to the amount of skepticism and change that any social system can absorb. Many of the Sophists taught their pupils techniques of debating and getting ahead, while questioning the traditional doctrines of religion, patriotism, and dedication to the welfare of the community. One of them is described by Plato as advocating the maxim that might makes right. In other words, the Sophists as a whole stimulated an attitude of doubt, relativism, and ambitious individualism, thereby contributing to the dissolution of the polis spirit.

**Socrates (469–399)** | Socrates, the patron saint of intellectuals, was at once a part of this movement and an opponent of it. During the troubled years of the Peloponnesian War he wandered the streets of Athens teaching his followers to test their beliefs and preconceptions with the tool of reason. "An uncriticized life," he observed, "is scarcely worth living." Like the Sophists he was interested in human rather than cosmic matters, but unlike many of them he was dissatisfied merely with tearing down traditional beliefs. He cleared the ground by posing seemingly innocent questions to his listeners that invariably entangled them in a hopeless maze of contradictions; but having devastated their opinions he substituted closely-reasoned conclusions of his own on the subject of ethics and the good life. Knowledge, he taught, was synonymous with virtue, for a person who knew the truth would act righteously. Impelled by this optimistic conviction, he continued to attack cherished beliefs—to play the role of "gadfly" as he put it.

Gadflies have seldom been popular. The Athenians, put on edge by their defeat at Sparta's hands (which was hastened by the treachery of one of Socrates' pupils) could at last bear him no longer. In 399 he was brought to trial for denying the gods and corrupting youth and was condemned by a close vote. In accordance with Athenian law, he was given the opportunity to propose his own punishment. He suggested that the Athenians punish him by giving him free meals at public expense for the rest of his life. By refusing to take the business seriously, he was in effect condemning himself to death. Declining an opportunity to escape into exile, he was executed by poison. He expired with the cheerful observation that at last he had the opportunity of discovering for himself the truth about the afterlife.

**Plato (427-347)** | Socrates would not have made good on an American university faculty, for although he was a splendid teacher, he did not publish.* We know of his teachings largely through the works of his student Plato, one of history's towering intellects and a prolific and graceful writer. In his *Republic,* Plato outlined the perfect polis—the first utopia in literary history. Here, ironically, the philosopher rejected the democracy that he knew and described an ideal state far more Spartan than Athenian. The farmers, workers, and merchants were without political rights; a warrior class was trained with Spartan rigor to defend the state; and an intellectual elite, schooled in mathematics and philosophy, constituted a ruling class. At the top of the political pyramid was a philosopher-king, the wisest and most virtuous product of a state-training program that consumed the better part of his life. Culture was not encouraged in the Republic; dangerous and novel ideas were banned, poets were banished, all music was prohibited except the martial, patriotic type.

What are we to make of a utopia that would encourage Sousa but ban Brahms—a polis that could never have pro-

---

*Jesus would have been denied tenure on the same grounds.

duced a Plato? We must remember that democratic Athens
was in decline when Plato wrote. He could not love the polis
that had executed his master, nor was he blind to the selfish individualism and civic irresponsibility that characterized fourth-
century Greece. Plato had the wit to recognize that through
the intensity of its cultural creativity and the freedom and
breadth of its intellectual curiosity the polis was burning itself out. Achilles had chosen a short but glorious life; Plato
preferred long mediocrity, and stability was therefore the
keynote of his Republic. There would be no Sophists to
erode civic virtue, no poets to exalt the individual over the
community (or abandon their shields as they fled from
battle). Plato's cavalier treatment of the mercantile classes
represents a deliberate rejection of the lures of empire. Like a
figure on a Grecian urn, his ideal polis would be frozen and
rigid—and enduring.

There remains the paradox that this intellectually static
commonwealth was to be ruled by philosophers. We tend to
think of philosophy as a singularly disputatious subject, but
Plato viewed truth as absolute and unchanging. He assumed
that all true philosophers would be in essential agreement—
that future thinkers would simply affirm Plato's own doctrines.

This assumption has proven to be resoundingly false, yet
Plato's conception of reality has nevertheless exerted an enormous influence on the development of thought. His purpose
was to reconcile his belief in a perfect, unchanging universe
with the diversity and impermanence of the visible world. He
stated that the objects that we perceive through our senses
are merely pale, imperfect reflections of ideal models or
archetypes that exist in a world invisible to us. For example,
we observe numerous individual cats, some black, some yellow, some fat, some skinny. All are imperfect particulariza-
tions of an ideal cat existing in the Platonic heaven. Again,
we find in the world of the senses many examples of duality:
twins, lovers, pairs of jackasses, and so forth, but they merely
exemplify, more or less inadequately, the idea of "two"

which, in its pure state, is invisible and intangible. We cannot see "two". We can only see two *things*. But—and this is all important—we can *conceive* of "twoness" or abstract duality. Likewise, with sufficient effort, we can conceive of "catness," "dogness" and "rabbitness"—of the archetypal cat, dog or rabbit. If we could not, so Plato believes, we would have no basis for grouping individual cats into a single category.

In short, the world of phenomena is not the *real* world. The phenomenal world is variegated and dynamic; the real world—the world of archetypes—is clear-cut and static. We can discover this real world through introspection, for knowledge of the archetypes is present in our minds from birth, dimly remembered from a previous existence. (Plato believed in a beforelife as well as in an afterlife.) So the philosopher studies reality not by observing but by thinking.

Plato illustrates this doctrine with a vivid metaphor. Imagine, he says, a cave whose inhabitants are chained in such a position that they can never turn toward the sunlit opening but can only see shadows projected against an interior wall. Imagine further that one of the inhabitants (the philosopher) breaks his chains, emerges from the cave, and sees the real world for the first time. He will have no wish to return to his former shadow world, but he will do so nevertheless out of a sense of obligation to enlighten the others. Similarly, the philosopher-king rules the Republic unwillingly through a sense of duty. He would prefer to contemplate reality undisturbed. Yet he alone can rule wisely, for he alone has seen the truth.

Plato's doctrine of ideas has always been alluring to people who seek order and unity, stability and virtue, in a universe that appears fickle and chaotic. Plato declared that the greatest of the archetypes is the idea of the Good, and this notion has had great appeal to people of religious temperament ever since. His theory of knowledge, emphasizing contemplation over observation, is obviously hostile to the method of experimental science, yet his archetypal world is perfectly compatible with the world of the mathematician—the world of pure numbers. Plato drew heavily from the Pythagorean tradition—"God is a geometer," he once observed—and Platonic thought, like Pythagorean thought, has contributed profoundly to the development of mathematical science. As for philosophy, it developed over the next two thousand years in the shadow of two giants. One of them is Plato; the other, Aristotle, Plato's greatest pupil.

**Aristotle (384–322)** | Plato founded a school in Athens called the Academy (from which arises our word, *academic*). To this school came the young Aristotle, the son of a Greek physician in the service of the king of Macedon. Aristotle remained at the Academy for nearly two decades. Then, after serving at the Macedonian court as tutor to Alexander the Great, he returned to Athens, founded a school of his own (the Lyceum), and wrote most of his books. At length he was condemned by the Athenians for "impiety" and escaped into exile, explaining as he fled that he wished to spare the Athenians from "a second sin against philosophy." He died shortly thereafter, in 322, one year after the death of Alexander. Thus Aristotle's life corresponds to the final phase of Classical Greece.

Aristotle was nearly a universal scholar. He wrote definitively on a great variety of topics including biology, politics, literature, ethics, logic, physics, and metaphysics. He brought Plato's theory of ideas down to earth by asserting that the archetype exists in the particular—that one can best study the archetypal cat by observing and classifying individual cats. Thus observation of things in this world takes its place alongside contemplation as a valid avenue to knowledge. Like Hippocrates and Thucydides, but on a much broader scale, Aristotle advocated the painstaking collection and analysis of data, thereby placing himself at odds with the main body of Greek thought. Although his political studies included the designing of an ideal commonwealth, he also investigated and classified the political systems of many existing poleis and demonstrated that several different types were conducive to the good life. His splendid biological studies followed the same method of observation and classification, and he set forth the concepts of genus and species which, with modifications, are still used. His work on physics has been less durable since it was based on an erroneous concept of motion, a fundamental belief in *purpose* as the organizing factor in the material universe, and an emphasis on qualitative rather than quantitative differences (for example, that the heavenly bodies were more perfect than objects on the earth). Mathematics had no genuine role in his system; in general, modern science draws its experimental method from the Aristotelian tradition and its mathematical analysis from the Pythagorean-Platonic tradition.

Aristotle's physics and metaphysics were based on the concept of a single God who was the motive power behind the universe—the unmoved mover and the uncaused cause to which all motion and all causation must ultimately be referred. Hence, Aristotolian thought was able to serve as a philosophical framework for later Islamic and Christian thought. Aristotle's immense significance in intellectual history arises from his having done some of the best thinking up to his time in so many significant realms of thought. It was he who first set forth a systematic logic, who first (so far as we know) produced a rigorous, detailed physics, who literally founded biology. A pioneer in observational method, he has been criticized for basing conclusions on insufficient evidence. Even Aristotle was not immune to the tendency toward premature conclusions, yet he collected data as no Greek before him had done. His achievement, considered in its totality, is without parallel in the history of thought.

Plato and Aristotle represent the apex of Greek philosophy. Both were religious men—both, in fact, were monotheists at heart. But both were dedicated also to the life of reason. Building on a rational heritage that had only begun in the sixth century, both produced philosophical systems of unparalleled sophistication and depth. Their thought climaxed the intellectual revolution that brought such glory and such turmoil to Greece.

# 9

## The Culture of
## the Golden Age

History has never seen anything like the intense cultural creativity of fifth-century Athens. It has been suggested that the
Athenians of the Golden Age were incapable of producing
anything ugly or vulgar; every surviving work of art, from the
greatest temple to the simplest ornament, was created with
unerring taste and assurance. Emotions ran strong and deep,
but they were controlled by a sure sense of form that never
permitted ostentation yet never degenerated into formalism.
The art of the period was an incarnation of the Greek maxim:
"nothing in excess"—a perfect embodiment of the taut balance and controlled excitement that we call "the classical
spirit."

Classical Greek culture was a product of the liberty and
dynamism of the polis. Compared to the sluggish societies of
the Near East, the world of the polis was intense and fluid.
Political systems, philosophical concepts, and artistic styles
evolved furiously. Aristocracies fell, tyrannies flourished, and
democracies were born in an atmosphere of social upheaval
and acute political awareness. The citizens of the Greek

poleis recognized that they were a people apart and that what separated them most fundamentally from their predecessors and contemporaries was their freedom. Herodotus describes Greeks as speaking to a Persian official in these words: "A slave's life you understand, but never having tasted liberty you cannot tell whether it be sweet or not. Had you known what freedom is, you would have bidden us fight for it," And the whole Persian War becomes for Herodotus an epic struggle between slavery and freedom.

It is not difficult to understand how Greek citizens, whose freedom far exceeded that of any previous civilized people, produced such a dynamic culture. It is less easy to explain the harmony and restraint of Greek classicism, for no people had ever before lived with such intensity and fervor. Herodotus tells us that even the barbaric Scythians lamented the Greek impulse toward frenzy, and a speaker in Thucydides observes that the Athenians "were born into the world to take no rest themselves and to give none to others." The Greek ideal was moderation and restraint precisely because these were the qualities most needed by an immoderate and unrestrained people. A degree of cooperation and self-control was essential to the communal life of the polis, and civic devotion acted as a brake on rampant individualism. During its greatest years the polis stimulated individual creativity but directed it toward the welfare of the community. Individualism and civic responsibility achieved a momentary and precarious balance.

The achievement of this equilibrium in the fifth century was a precious but fleeting episode in the evolution of the polis from the aristocratic conservatism of the previous age to the irresponsible individualism of the fourth century and thereafter, hastened by the growth of religious doubt and the tendency toward specialization. This process is illustrated clearly in the evolution of Greek art from the delicate, static elegance of the "archaic style" through the serious, balanced classical style of the fifth century to the increasing individualism, naturalism and particularism of the late-classical fourth century. In sculpture, for example, one observes a development from aristocratic stiffness to a harmonious serenity that gradually displays signs of increasing tension and individualization. The works of the fifth-century sculptors were idealized men—we might almost say Platonic archetypes. The fourth-century sculptors tended to abandon the archetype for the specific and the concrete. In short, as Greek life was evolving from civic allegiance to individualism, from traditionalism to self-expression, from aristocracy to democracy, there was a moment when these opposites were balanced—and the moment was frozen and immortalized in some of the most superb works of architecture, sculpture, and dramatic literature the world has known.

The Golden Age of Greece was the Golden Age of Athens, for the wealth of empire and the ambitious building program of Pericles drew talent from throughout the Greek world. Periclean Athens had a long artistic tradition behind it and a buoyant self-assurance that was born at Marathon, confirmed at Salamis, and heightened by a successful career in imperialism. But the Athenian Golden Age was expensive to the rest of Greece in both money and talent. It is interesting that at its cultural zenith the Greek polis system had already evolved a good distance from the original ideal of the independent self-contained state. Athens was not merely a polis; she was an empire. And although the civic spirit was the key element in Athenian culture, imperial trade and imperial tribute paid the bills. The culture of the Golden Age is unquestionably a polis culture, but it is the culture of a polis in the process of losing its innocence.

The Golden Age of Pericles rested not only on economic foundations of imperial tribute but on slavery as well. This fact should not be exaggerated; slavery was the basis of most ancient cultures. But it cannot be overlooked.

**Athenian Life** | In Periclean Athens individualism was still strongly oriented toward the polis. One of the basic differences between the daily life of the fifth-century Athenian

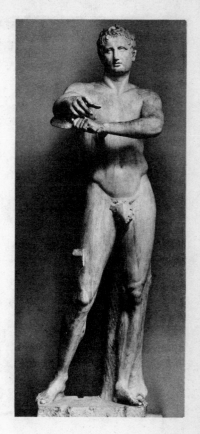

Maiden dressed in a Dorian gar-
ment, about 530 B.C.; an example of the archaic style (*Marburg
—Art Reference Bureau, Acropolis Museum*).

Apoxyomenos (scraper); Roman
marble copy probably of bronze
original by Lysippus, about 330
B.C. (*Vatican Museum*).

citizen and that of the modern American is the Athenian's
emphasis on public over private affairs. The private life of
even the most affluent Athenian was rigorously simple: his
clothing was plain, his home was humble, his furniture was
rudimentary. With the intensification of individualism in the
fourth century, private homes became much more elaborate,
but during the Golden Age the Athenian's private life was, by
our standards, almost as Spartan as the Spartan's.

Discobolus (discus thrower); Roman marble copy of bronze original by
Myron, about 450 B.C. (*Vatican Museum*).

The plainness of private life was counterbalanced, however, by the brilliant diversity of public life. Under Pericles,
imperial Athens lavished its wealth and genius on its own
adornment. The great works of art and architecture were
dedicated to the polis and its gods. Life was enriched by the
pageantry of civic religious festivals, by spirited conversation
in the market-place (the agora), by exercise in elaborate civic
gymnasiums complete with baths and dressing rooms, and of
course by participation in political affairs. The Greeks social-
ized the amenities of life; the pursuit of excellence in body

and mind, so typical of Greek culture, was carried on in a communal atmosphere. The good life was not the life of the individual but the life of the citizen.

Not everybody in Athens was a citizen. Women, slaves, children, and metics (resident aliens) were all excluded from the privileges of citizenship. Although many metics prospered in business, many slaves were well-treated, and many women had loving husbands, only the citizens could participate fully in the life of the polis. Aristotle sought to give rational sanction to this state of affairs by proving (to his own satisfaction) that slaves and women were naturally inferior beings. The citizen's wife in Periclean Athens remained in the home. She had heavy domestic duties but few social responsibilities and was legally under her husband's control. Since her education was confined to the level of "home economics," her husband was not likely to find her especially interesting. At the parties and festive gatherings of the citizens the only women present were foreigners, often Ionians, who were more notable for their charm and wit than for their virtue. Typical of these women was Pericles' mistress, Aspasia, a sophisticated, well-educated Ionian whose name, appropriately enough, means "welcome." The wives of Athens were denied the rich public life of the Golden Age, and their lot is expressed eloquently in one of the tragedies of Euripides: "For a man may go, when home life palls, to join with friends and raise his spirits in companionship. But for us poor wives it is solitary communion with the one same soul forever."

**Greek Drama** | The civic culture of the Golden Age achieved its most notable triumphs in drama, architecture, and sculpture. All three illustrate the public orientation of Greek cultural life. Greek tragedy arose out of the worship of Dionysus, as the songs and dances of the worshipers gradually evolved into a formalized drama with actors and a chorus. The sixth-century Athenian tyrant Pisistratus gave vigorous support to the Dionysian drama, and by the fifth century it had become a great civic institution. Wealthy citizens were expected to finance the productions, and each year a body of civic judges would award prizes to the three best tragedies.

By modern standards the performances were far from elaborate. The most important of them took place in an outdoor "Theater of Dionysus" on the southern slope of the Acropolis. The chorus sang and danced to a simple musical accompaniment and commented at intervals on the action of the drama. Behind the chorus were low, broad steps on which the actors performed. There were never more than three actors on the stage at one time, and the sets behind them were simple in the extreme. The dramas themselves were based on mythological or historical themes, often dealing with semi-legendary royal families of early Greece, but the playwrights went beyond the realm of historical narrative to probe deeply some of the fundamental problems of morality and religion.

The immense popularity of these stark, profound, and uncompromising productions testifies to the remarkable cultural elevation of fifth-century Athens. The citizens who flocked to the Theater of Dionysus constituted a critical and sophisticated audience. Many had themselves participated in the numerous dramas that were constantly being performed both in the city and in the surrounding Attican countryside. It has been estimated that each year some 3000 citizens had the experience of performing in a dramatic chorus, and thousands more had been trained, as a part of the normal Athenian curriculum, in singing, dancing, declamation, and acting. The drama was a central and meaningful element in the life of the polis and serves as an added illustration of the many-sidedness of human experience in the Golden Age.

The three great tragedians of fifth-century Athens were Aeschylus, who wrote during the first half of the century; Sophocles, whose productive period covered the middle and later decades of the century; and Euripides, a younger contemporary of Sophocles. All three exemplify the seriousness, the order, the controlled tension that we identify as "classical," yet they also illustrate the changes the classical spirit was undergoing. Aeschylus, the first of the three, tended to emphasize traditional values. Deeply devoted to the polis and the Greek religious heritage, he probed with majestic dignity the fundamental relationships of man and his gods, the problem of injustice in a righteous universe, and the terrible consequences of overweening pride.

Sophocles was less intellectually rigorous and less traditional than Aeschylus. But he was a supreme dramatic artist with an unerring sense of plot structure and characterization. His plays treat the most violent and agonizing emotional situations with restraint and sobriety. In Sophocles the perfect classical equilibrium is fully achieved. Never have passions been so intense yet under such masterly control.

The younger dramatist Euripides displays the logic, the skepticism, and the hard-headed rationalism of the Sophists who were then the rage of Athens. One of his characters makes the audacious statement, "There are no gods in heaven; no, not one!" And Euripides, far more than his predecessors, demonstrated a deep, sympathetic understanding of the hopes and fears, the unpredictability and irrationality, and the *individuality* of human nature. Aeschylus' characters were chiefly types rather than individuals; in Sophocles the individual emerges with much greater clarity; but Euripides portrays his characters with insight and psychological realism. With the tragedies of Euripides the new age of skepticism and acute individualism has dawned.

The depth and power of fifth-century tragedy is exemplified in Sophocles' *Antigone*, which deals with the perennial conflict between individual conscience and state authority. Antigone's brother has betrayed his country and has been killed. Her uncle, the king of Thebes, refuses to permit her brother's burial even though burial was regarded as mandatory in the Greek religious tradition. Torn by the conflict between the royal decree and her sense of religious obligation, Antigone defies the king, buries her brother, and is condemned to death. She addresses the king in these words:

I did not think that thy decrees were of such force as to override
the unwritten and unfailing laws of heaven. For their duration is
not of today or yesterday, but from eternity; and no man knows
when they were first put forth. And though men rage I must obey
those laws. Die I must, for death must come to all. But if I am to
die before my time, I'll do it gladly; for when one lives as I do,
surrounded by evils, death can only be a gain. So death for me is
but a trifling grief, far better than to let my mother's son lie an
unburied corpse.

The lighter side of the fifth-century theater is represented
by the great comic playwright Aristophanes who, taking advantage of the freedom of the Athenian theater, subjected his
fellow citizens great and small to merciless ridicule as he exposed the pretensions and follies of imperial Athens during
the Peloponnesian War. A product of the age of Socrates and
the Sophists, Aristophanes expressed his deep-rooted conservatism by lampooning them. Socrates appears in a comedy
called *The Clouds* hanging from a basket suspended in the air
so that he could contemplate the heavens at closer range,
while his students below studied geology, their noses in the
earth and their posteriors upraised toward the sky. Aristophanes was an ardent pacifist who condemned Athenian participation in the Peloponnesian War and mocked the war leaders
with a frankness that would seldom be tolerated by a modern
democracy during wartime. The audacity of his criticism
illustrates the degree of intellectual freedom that existed in
fifth-century Athens. Yet his plays also betray a yearning for
the dignity and traditionalism of former years and a disturb-
ing conviction that all was not well.

**Architecture and Sculpture** | Every aspect of fifth-century
culture displays the classical spirit of restrained excitement.
We find it in Athenian drama where the most violent deeds
and passions are presented in an ordered and unified framework. We find it in the history of Thucydides, who treats
with dispassionate analysis the impetuous and often childish
excesses of the Peloponnesian War. And we find it in the
architecture and art of fifth-century Athens: deeply moving

yet balanced and controlled. When Xerxes burned the Acropolis he left the next generation of Athenians with a challenge and an opportunity: to rebuild the temples in the new, classical style—to crown the polis with structures of such majesty and perfection as the world had never seen. Athenian imperialism provided the money with which to rebuild, and Pericles, against the opposition of a conservative minority, pursued a lavish policy of civic beautification as a part of his effort to make Athens the cultural center of Hellas. The age of Pericles was therefore a period of feverish public building; its supreme architectural monument was the central temple on the reconstructed Acropolis—the Parthenon. This structure, dedicated to the patron goddess Athena, is the ultimate expression of the classical ideal. It creates its effect not from a sense of fluidity and upward-reaching, as in the much later Gothic cathedral, but from a superb harmony of proportions. Here indeed was "nothing in excess."

The genius of the architects was matched by that of the sculptors who decorated the temples and created the great statues that were placed inside them. The most distinguished of the fifth-century sculptors was Phidias, the master sculptor of the Parthenon, who was responsible either directly or through his helpers for its splendid reliefs. Phidias made a majestic statue of Athena in ivory and gold for the interior of the Parthenon and a still larger statue of the same goddess which was placed in the open and could be seen by ships several miles at sea.

The work of Phidias and his contemporaries comes at the great moment of classical balance. Their works portray human beings as types, without individual problems or cares, vigorous yet serene, ideally proportioned, and often in a state of controlled tension.

The architecture and sculpture of the Parthenon and its surrounding temples exemplify perfectly the synthesis of religious feeling, patriotic dedication, artistic genius, and intellectual freedom that characterized the age of Pericles. It would be pleasant to think of the Athenians of this period

The Acropolis of Athens (*Alinari—Art Reference Bureau*).

The Parthenon (*Marburg—Art Reference Bureau*).

Head of the Athena Lemnia; after Pheidias (*Alinari—Art Reference Bureau, Civic Museum Bologna*).

enjoying the beauty of these temples that so wonderfully express the mood of the age. But such was not the case. The Parthenon, the first of the Acropolis structures to be completed, was not finished until 432, a scant year before the outbreak of the Peloponnesian War that ultimately brought Athens to her knees. By 432 the old civic-religious enthusiasm was already waning. For centuries after, Greek art would be a living, creative thing; indeed, some of its most illustrious masterpieces were products of these later centuries. But the balanced, confident spirit of Periclean Athens—the spirit that informed the works of Sophocles and Phidias and inspired the Parthenon—could never quite be recovered.

# 10

---

# The Hellenistic Age

**Alexander the Great** | The decline of the polis in the fourth century culminated, as we have seen, in the triumphs of King Philip and the subordination of Greece to the power of Macedon. In 336 B.C., barely two years after his climactic victory over Athens and Thebes at Chaeronea, Philip of Macedon was murdered as a consequence of a palace intrigue. He was succeeded by his son, Alexander, later to be called "the Great."

In his final months Philip had been preparing a large-scale attack against the Persian Empire. His hope was to transform the grudging obedience of the Greek city-states into enthusiastic support by leading a Pan-Hellenic crusade against the traditional enemy of Hellas. Alexander, during a dazzling reign of thirteen years, exceeded his father's most fantastic dreams. Leading his all-conquering armies from Greece to India, he changed the course of the ancient world.

Although only twenty when he inherited the throne, Alexander possessed in the fullest measure that combination of physical attractiveness, athletic prowess, and intellectual distinction which had always been the Greek ideal. He had a godly countenance, the physique of an Olympian athlete, and a penetrating, imaginative mind. He was a magnetic leader who inspired intense loyalty and admiration among his followers, a brilliant general who adapted his tactics and strategy to the most varied circumstances, and an ardent champion of Hellenic culture and the Greek way of life. He was the product of two great teachers: Aristotle, the master philosopher and universal intellect, and King Philip himself, the best general and most adroit political opportunist of the age. Alexander's turn of mind is symbolized by the two objects that he always kept beneath his pillow: the *Iliad* and a dagger.

At first the Greek city-states were restive under Alexander's rule. He quelled their revolts with merciless efficiency, destroying rebellious Thebes and frightening the rest into submission. But there was genuine support for his campaign against the Persian Empire. In the spring of 334 B.C. he led a Greco-Macedonian army of some 40,000 men across the Dardanelles into Asia Minor, and, during the next three and one-half years, won a series of stunning victories over the aged and ramshackle Persian Empire. He freed the Ionian cities from Persian control and conquered the imperial provinces of Syria and Egypt. Then, striking deep into the heart of the Empire, he won a decisive victory over the unwieldy Persian army near Arbela on the Tigris in 331. The triumph at Arbela enabled Alexander to seize the vast imperial treasure, ascend the imperial throne, and bring an end to the dynasty of ancient Persia.

This was a glorious moment for the Greeks. The foe that had so long troubled Hellas was conquered. More than that, the ancient Near East was now under Greek control, open to the influence of Greek enterprise, Greek culture and Greek rationalism. Alexander's conquest of Persia set the stage for a new epoch—a period known as the *Hellenistic Age* as distinct from the previous *Classical Age*. The Greeks were now the masters of the ancient world, and under their rule a great cosmopolitan culture developed, distinctly Greek in tradition yet transmuted by the influence of the subject oriental civilizations and by the spacious new environment in which the Greeks now lived.

The Hellenization of the Near East was stimulated by Alexander's policy of founding cities in the wake of his conquests and filling them with Greek settlers. These communities, although intended chiefly as military and commercial bases, became islands of Greek culture which were often able to exert a powerful influence on the surrounding area. Most of them were named, immodestly, after their founder. The greatest of them by far was Alexandria in Egypt which Alexander founded at the mouth of the Nile. Alexandria quickly outstripped the cities of Greece itself to become the great commercial center of the Hellenistic world, and before long it had developed a cultural and intellectual life that put contemporary Athens to shame.

No sooner had he ascended the throne of Persia than Alexander began preparations for further campaigns. The final seven years of his life were occupied in conquering the easternmost provinces of the Persian Empire and pushing on into India, impelled by an insatiable thirst for conquest and by the lure of undiscovered lands. His spirit and ingenuity were taxed to the utmost by the variety of difficulties that he encountered: the rugged mountains of Afghanistan, the hostile stretches of the Indus Valley, fierce armies equipped with hundreds of elephants. At length his own army, its endurance exhausted, refused to go further. Alexander returned to central Persia in 323 where, in the midst of organizing his immense empire, he fell ill and died, perhaps of malaria, at the age of thirty-two.

The empire of Alexander was the greatest that the world had ever seen—more extensive even than the Persian Empire. Wherever he went Alexander adapted himself to the customs of the land. He ruled Egypt as a divine pharaoh and Persia as an Oriental despot, demanding that his subjects prostrate themselves in his presence. (His Greek followers objected vigorously to this.) He married the daughter of the last Persian emperor and urged his countrymen to follow his example by taking wives from among the Persian aristocracy. His goal was apparently nothing less than a homogeneous Greco-Oriental empire—a fusion of East and West. To what extent this policy was the product of deliberate calculation, to what extent a consequence of his intoxication with the splendors of the ancient Orient will never be known. But the project was scarcely underway when Alexander died, leaving behind him a sense of loss and bewilderment and a vast state that nobody but a second Alexander could have held together.

**The Successor States** | The empire was divided among the generals of Alexander's staff, who founded a series of Macedonian dynasties that ruled Greece and most of the ancient Near East until the Roman conquests of the second and first centuries B.C. There was great conflict over the division of the spoils, and for several decades after Alexander's death the political situation remained fluid. But in broad outline the succession went as follows: Ptolemy, one of Alexander's ablest generals, ruled Egypt, establishing the Ptolemaic dynasty that lasted until a Roman army deposed Cleopatra, the last of the Ptolemies, in 30 B.C. From Alexandria, their magnificent capital, the Ptolemies ruled with all the pomp and severity of the most powerful pharaohs, enriching themselves by merciless exploitation of the peasantry and suppressing all political activities, even among the multitudes of Greeks in Alexandria. The capital, with its imposing public buildings, its superb library and museum, its far flung commerce, and its million inhabitants was the wonder of the age. But elsewhere Egypt remained essentially unchanged except for a growing hostility toward the authoritarianism of the Greek regime.

Northern Syria and most of the remaining provinces of the old Persian Empire fell to another of Alexander's generals, Seleucus, who founded the Seleucid dynasty. The kingdom of the Seleucids was far more heterogeneous and loosely organized than that of the Ptolemies, and as time went on cer-

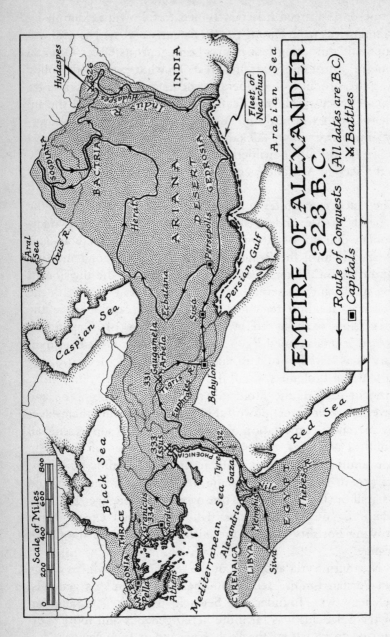

Empire of Alexander, 323 B.C.

tain of the more self-conscious Near Eastern peoples began to
rebel against the Seleucid policy of Hellenization. This was
particularly true of the Persians and Jews who had each produced powerful transcendental religions and resented bitterly
the influx of Greek religious thought. Farther to the east, the
more remote provinces of the Persian Empire gradually fell
away from Seleucid control. The center of Seleucid power
was the city of Antioch in northern Syria, second only to
Alexandria in population, wealth, and opulence.

The third important successor state, Macedon, passed into
the hands of a dynasty known as the Antigonids, whose authority over the Greek poleis to the south was never very
firm and whose power was usually inferior to that of the
Ptolemies and Seleucids. A number of smaller states also developed out of the wreckage of Alexander's empire, but the
three dominant successor kingdoms were Antigonid Greece,
Seleucid Asia, and Ptolemaic Egypt.

**The Change In Mood** | These huge political agglomerations
now replaced the small city-states as the typical units of the
Greek world. The new environment provided vast opportunities and encouraged a sense of cosmopolitanism that contrasts with the provincialism of the polis. This was a prosperous age, an age of vigorous and profitable business activity
and successful careers in commerce and banking. The good
life was reserved, however, for the fortunate few. Slavery
continued, even increased, and the peasants and urban commoners were kept at an economic level of bare subsistence.
The typical agrarian unit was no longer the small or middle-
sized farm but the large plantation worked by slaves.

The poleis in Greece itself retained throughout the new age
a portion of their earlier autonomy. Old civic institutions
continued to function and citizens still had a voice in domestic politics. But the Greek peninsula was now an economic
backwater, and cities like Athens and Thebes were overshadowed by the new superstates. Ambitious Greeks were lured
by opportunity far from their homeland, as they had once

been lured to imperial Athens. No longer involved in political affairs or in the intense life of a free community, the overseas Greek found himself adrift in a wide and bewildering world over which he had no control.

The cosmopolitanism of the Hellenistic age was accompanied by a sense of estrangement and alienation, of uncertainty, loneliness, and impotence. The trend toward extreme individualism, professionalism, and specialization which we have already observed in the fourth century was enormously accelerated. The impulse toward greater realism and individualism in sculpture was pushed to its limits, and many Hellenistic sculptors turned to portraying the bizarre and the grotesque— ugliness, deformity, agony, and old age—sometimes with exceedingly effective results. The civic consciousness of the comic playwright Aristophanes in the fifth century gave way to the highly individualized and superficial realism of the Hellenistic drawing-room comedy and bedroom farce. The Hellenistic Age produced superb works of art, but they lacked the serenity and balance of the earlier period. Whether this fact detracts from their artistic merit or adds to it is a matter of taste, but they are obviously products of a radically different society—still brilliant, still intensely creative, but anchorless.

**Religion And Ethics** | Hellenic religion, with its traditional civic orientation, was all but transformed in this new age. Ancient bonds and loyalties were broken as many adventurous Greeks were uprooted from their poleis and thrown on their own. The result was a mood of intense individualism which found expression in a variety of religious and ethical ideas stressing personal fulfillment or personal salvation rather than involvement in the community. Individualism and cosmopolitanism went hand in hand, for as the Greek abdicated spiritually from the polis and retired into himself, he came to regard all humanity as a multitude of individuals—a universal brotherhood in which intelligent Persians, Egyptians, and Jews were no worse than intelligent Greeks. The traditional con-

Old Market Woman: Hellenistic realism, second century B.C. (*The Metropolitan Museum of Art, Rogers Fund, 1909*).

trast between Greek and barbarian faded, for it had been the free spirit of the polis that had set the Greek apart, and the polis, in its traditional sense, was now becoming an anachronism. Yet the concept of cosmopolis, the idea of human brotherhood, was too abstract to provide the sense of involvement and orientation that the polis had formerly given. The root-

Laocoön, late second century B.C.; sculpture shows Laocoön and his sons struggling with snakes (*Alinari—Art Reference Bureau, Vatican Museum*).

less Greek tended to turn away from his old Olympic gods and seek solace in more personal and potent religious concepts. Hellenistic religion is characterized by a withdrawal from active social participation—a search for sanctuary in a restless and uncertain world.

The Hellenistic age saw a vigorous revival of mystery and salvation cults such as Orphism and the worship of Dionysus
and Demeter which had always lurked behind the Olympic
foreground. And various Near Eastern mystery religions now
became popular among the Greeks. Almost all of these were
centered on the death and resurrection of a god and the
promise of personal salvation. From Egypt came the cult of
Osiris who died, was reborn, and now sat in judgment of the
dead. From Asia Minor came a version of the ancient and
widespread fertility cult of the Great Mother. Form Persia,
somewhat later, came the cult of Mithras, a variation of Zoroastrianism, which added to the traditional concept of a cosmic struggle between good and evil the idea of a savior-hero
who redeemed mankind.

Alongside these and other oriental cults came a revival of
neo-Babylonian astrology, of magic, witchcraft, and sorcery.
Many ambitious men of the upper class were devoted to the
goddess of Fortune who rewarded talent and ambition and
brought her worshipers material well-being. The Hellenistic
world became a religious melting pot in which a single individual might be a devotee of several cults. Many thoughtful
people adopted the idea of "syncretism," that is, the notion
that the gods of different peoples are actually various manifestations of the same god—that Zeus, Osiris, even Yahweh,
all symbolize a single divine spirit. (The more orthodox
among the Jews found this doctrine abominable.) Religious
beliefs and religious attitudes throughout the Hellenistic
world were tending to become homogenized, thereby preparing the soil for the later triumph of Christianity.

**Skeptics, Cynics, Stoics, And Epicureans** | Many Greeks of
the post-Classical age turned neither to the old Orphic and
Dionysian cults nor to the salvation cults of the Orient but
sought to adapt elements of the Hellenic intellectual tradition
to the new conditions. One group, the Skeptics, intensified
the relativism of the Sophists by denying the possibility of
any knowledge whatever, either of gods, men, or nature. The

human mind, they maintained, is incapable of apprehending reality (if, indeed, there is any such thing as "reality"), and all beliefs and statements of fact are equally unverifiable. In doubting everything they carried rationalism to its ultimate, self-destructive limit and reflected the profound uncertainty of the new age.

Another group, the Cynics, demonstrated in various forms of eccentric behavior their contempt for conventional piety and patriotism and their rebellion against the hypocrisy that they detected in the lives and attitudes of their contemporaries. Diogenes, the most famous of the Cynics, was something of a fourth-century hippie who sought integrity in a world of careerists and phonies. He rejected all official and traditional religions, all participation in civic life, marriage, the public games, and the theater. He ridiculed the prestige that was associated with wealth, power, and reputation and honored instead the simple life of courage, reason, and honesty—a life of virtue—which could best be attained by a rejection of civilization and a return to nature. The man of integrity, the wise and honest man, should live like a dog, without pretensions and uncluttered by worldly possessions. Indeed, the very word *cynic* originally meant *canine* or "doglike." So Diogenes wandered the streets begging for his food, a homeless but free man. His bedchamber was a tub outside a temple of the Great Mother; his latrine was the public street. He obeyed no laws, recognized no polis, and became, next to Alexander, the most illustrious man of his age. He was a colorful symbol of the great Hellenistic withdrawal from the polis into the individual soul.

The same withdrawal is evident in the two religio-ethical systems that emerged in the fourth century and influenced human thought and conduct for centuries thereafter: Stoicism and Epicureanism. Both were philosophies of resignation that taught men to fortify their souls against the harshness of life. Zeno, the founder of the Stoic School, stressed, as the Cynics did, the vanity of worldly things and the supreme importance of individual virtue. Every man, whether statesman, artist, or peasant, should pursue his calling honestly and seriously. The significant thing, however, was not individual accomplishment but individual effort; such things as politics, art, and even farming were ultimately valueless, yet in pursuing them as best he could the individual manifested his virtue. Since virtue was all-important, the good Stoic was immune to the vicissitudes of life. He might lose his property; he might be imprisoned and tortured, but except by his own will he could not be deprived of his virtue—his only really precious possession. By rejecting the world the Stoic created an impenetrable citadel within his own soul. Out of this doctrine there emerged a sense not only of individualism but of cosmopolitanism; the idea of the polis faded before the wider Stoic concept of a brotherhood of men.

Ultimately the Stoic emphasis on virtue was rooted in a lofty cosmic vision based on the Greek conception of a rational, orderly, purposeful universe. The harmonious movements of the stars and planets and growth of complex plants from simple seeds all pointed to the existence of a Divine Plan, which was both intelligent and good. We humans were incapable of perceiving the details of the Plan as it worked in our own lives, yet by living virtuously and doing our best we could cooperate with it. The God of the universe cared about mankind, and the stern nobility of Stoic ethics was tempered and humanized by this optimistic assurance.

Epicurus, whose school was Stoicism's great rival, differed from Zeno both in his concept of human ethics and in his vision of the universe. He taught that man should seek happiness rather than virtue. Yet happiness to the Epicureans was not the pursuit of thrills and euphoria, but rather a quiet, balanced life. The life of the drunkard is saddened by countless hangovers, the life of the swinger by countless complications. Happiness is best achieved not by chasing pleasures but by living simply and unobtrusively, being kind and affectionate to one's friends, learning to endure pain when it comes, and avoiding needless fears. In short, good Epicureans did not differ noticeably from good Stoics in actual behavior, for virtue was the pathway to happiness. But the Epicureans rejected the optimistic Stoic doctrine of divine purpose. Epicurus followed the teachings of the atomists in viewing the universe not as a great hierarchy of cosmic spheres centering on the earth, but as a vast multiplicity of atoms much the same one place as another. Our world is not the handiwork of God, but a chance configuration. The gods, if they exist, care nothing for us, and we ought to draw from this fact the comforting conclusion that we need not fear them.

Epicureanism even more than Stoicism was a philosophy of withdrawal. It was a wise, compassionate teaching that sought to banish fear, curb passions, and dispel illusions, but its doctrine of happiness was too limited and too bland to stir the millions and convert empires. Yet through the lofty epic poetry of the Roman writer Lucretius (98–53 B.C.), it made its impact on the intellectual life of Rome. Although never as popular as Stoicism, it gave solace and direction, during the remaining centuries of antiquity, to an influential minority of wise and sensitive people.

**Hellenistic Science** | In the Hellenistic age, Greek science reached maturity. The naive generalizations of the earlier period gave way to a rigorous and highly creative professionalism. Aristotle's salutary example was followed and improved upon by the Hellenistic scientists who collected and sifted data with great thoroughness before framing their hypotheses.

Alexandria was the center of scientific thought in this age. Here the Ptolemies built and subsidized a great research center—the Museum of Alexandria—and collected a library of unprecedented size and diversity containing some half-million papyrus rolls. At Alexandria and elsewhere, science and mathematics made rapid strides as Greek rationalism encountered the rich, amorphous heritage of Near Eastern astrology, medical lore, and practical mathematics. The fruitful medical investigations of Hippocrates' school were carried on and expanded by Hellenistic physicians, particularly in Alexandria. Their pioneer work in the dissection of human bodies enabled them to discover the nervous system, to learn a great deal about the brain, heart, and arteries, and to perform successful surgical operations. In mathematics, Euclid organized plane and solid geometry into a systematic, integrated body of knowledge. Archimedes of Syracuse did brilliant original work in both pure and applied mathematics, discovering specific gravity, experimenting successfully with levers and pulleys to lift tremendous weights, and coming very close to the invention of calculus.

The wide-ranging military campaigns of Alexander and the subsequent cultural interchange between large areas of the world led to a vast increase in Greek geographical knowledge. Eratosthenes, the head of the Alexandrian Library in the later third century, produced the most accurate and thorough world maps that had yet been made, complete with lines of longitude and latitude and climatic zones. He recognized that the earth was a sphere and was even able to determine its circumference with an error of less than 1%. He did this by measuring the altitude of the sun at different latitudes, calculating from this data the length of one degree of latitude on the earth's surface, and multiplying the result by 360 (degrees).

The same painstaking accuracy and dazzling ingenuity is evident in the work of the Hellenistic astronomers. Aristarchus of Samos suggested that the earth rotated daily on its axis and revolved yearly around the sun. This heliocentric hypothesis is a startling anticipation of modern astronomical conclusions, but Aristarchus' erroneous assumption that the earth's motion around the sun was uniform and circular rendered his system inaccurate. Aristarchus' theory was never widely accepted because it failed to explain the precise astronomical observations then being made at Alexandria, and because it violated the hallowed doctrine of an earth-centered universe. Later the great Hellenistic astronomer Hipparchus developed a complex system of circles and subcircles centered on the earth, which accounted exceedingly well for the observed motions of the sun and moon. Hipparchus' ingenious system, expanded and perfected by the Alexandrian astronomer Ptolemy in the second century A.D., represents antiquity's final word on the subject—a comprehensive geometrical model of the universe that, although fundamentally wrong, corresponded satisfactorily to the best observations of the day. And it should be remembered that a scientific hypothesis must be judged not by some objective standard of rightness or wrongness but by its success in accounting for and predicting observed phenomena. By this criterion the Ptolemaic system stands as one of the impressive triumphs of Hellenistic thought.

**The Hellenistic Legacy** | Greek culture exerted a fundamental influence on the Roman Empire, the Byzantine and Muslim civilizations, and the medieval West; but it did so largely in its Hellenistic form. The conclusions of the Hellenistic philosophers and scholars tended to be accepted by the best minds of later ages, but the Hellenistic spirit of free inquiry and intellectual daring was not matched until the sixteenth and seventeenth centuries. There is something remarkably modern about the Hellenistic world with its confident scientists, its cosmopolitanism, its materialism, its religious diversity, its trend toward increasing specialization, its large-scale business activity, and its sense of drift and disorientation. But the Hellenistic social conscience remained dormant and Hellenistic economic organization, regardless of superficial similarities, was vastly different from ours. Based on human slavery rather than machines, it provided only a tiny fraction of the population with the benefits of its commerical prosperity. The great majority remained servile and illiterate.

Still, the upper classes throughout the Mediterranean world and the Near East were exposed to Greek culture and the Greek language, and the Greeks themselves were deeply influenced by Oriental thought. From Syria, Asia Minor, and the Nile valley to Magna Graecia in the West a common culture was developing with common ideas and common gods.

The way was being paved for the political unification of the Mediterranean world under the authority of Rome, and its spiritual unification under the Christian Church. Alexander's dream of a homogeneous Greco-Oriental world was gradually coming into being. But had Alexander foreseen the consequences of his handiwork—the conquest of Hellas by an Italian city and a Near Eastern faith—he might well have chosen to spend his days in seclusion.

## GREEK CHRONOLOGY

All Dates B.C.

| | |
|---|---|
| c.3000—1400: | Minoan civilization |
| c.1500—1120: | Mycenaean civilization |
| c.1200: | Trojan war |
| c.1200—1000: | Dorian invasions |
| c.1120—800: | "Dark Age" |
| c.750—550: | Era of colonization |
| c.650 ff.: | Rise of tyrants |
| c.594: | Solon reforms Athenian laws |
| c.582—507: | Pythagoras |
| 561—527: | Pisistratus rules Athens |
| 508: | Cleisthenes reforms Athenian laws |
| 490—479: | Persian Wars |
| 477: | Delian League established |
| c.460—429: | Era of Pericles |
| 454: | Delian treasury moved to Athens |
| 432: | Parthenon completed |
| 431—404: | Peloponnesian War |
| 469—399: | Socrates |
| 427—347: | Plato |
| 384—322: | Aristotle |
| 359—336: | Reign of Philip of Macedon |
| 338: | Battle of Chaeronea: Philip establishes mastery over Greece |
| 336—323: | Reign of Alexander the Great |
| 323 ff.: | The Hellenistic Age |

# PART TWO

# Suggested Readings

The asterisk indicates a paperback edition.

### Crete, Mycenae, and the Dark Age

Leonard Cottrell, *The Bull of Minos* (*Grosset and Dunlap). An entertaining account of Minoan-Mycenean archaeology.

John Chadwick, *The Decipherment of Linear B* (*Modern Library). A masterpiece of scholarship written by one of the key figures in the decipherment.

J. Forsdyke, *Greece Before Homer* (*Norton). Using mythology to reconstruct history, the author provides a fine introduction to the literary and archaeological records of prehistoric Greece.

Homer, *The Odyssey*, many translations. The most recent and perhaps the best is by Robert Fitzgerald (*Anchor).

Homer, *The Iliad*, many translations. We suggest the verse translation by Richmond Lattimore (*University of Chicago).

A. E. Samuel, *Mycenaeans in History* (*Prentice-Hall). A brief, lively, well-illustrated narrative of the Mycenaeans from Neolithic times to the flowering of their culture in the late Bronze Age.

H. J. Rose, *Handbook of Greek Mythology* (*Dutton). The best scholarly treatment of the subject.

Gilbert Murray, *Five Stages of Greek Religion* (*Anchor). A superb interpretive study, rationalist in orientation, covering the period from the beginnings through the later Roman Empire.

Frances Wilkes, *Ancient Crete* (*John Day). A good, recent account of Minoan civilization.

P. MacKendrick, *The Greek Stones Speak* (*Mentor). A nontechnical site-by-site description of archaeological investigations covering the Greek world to Roman times.

R. Higgins, *Minoan and Mycenaean Art* (*Praeger). An excellent, well-illustrated survey.

## The Rise of Classical Greece

J. B. Bury, *A History of Greece* (3rd ed., rev. by R. Meiggs, Macmillan). The best political survey, covers Greek history in detail to the death of Alexander.

H. D. F. Kitto, *The Greeks* (*Penguin). An illuminating and provocative interpretation of Greek history to Alexander written by an enthusiastic Phil-Hellene who finds little to criticize in ancient Hellas.

M. I. Finley, *The Ancient Greeks* (Viking). An excellent recent survey of Greek life and thought, brief but authoritative.

H. Lloyd-Jones, ed., *The Greeks* (World). A collection of scholarly essays, each by a specialist, stressing intellectual and culutral history.

W. G. Forrest, *History of Sparta* (*Hutchinson). A very brief but exemplary history, 950—192 B.C.

A. Andrews, *The Greek Tyrants* (*Harper). Concise, yet perhaps the best account of the age of the tyrants.

A. R. Burn, *The Lyric Age of Greece* (*Minerva). A comprehensive account, covering the political, social, military, scientific, philosophical and literary history of the period.

A. E. Zimmern, *The Greek Commonwealth* (*Oxford Galaxy). A classic study of political, economic, and social life in fifth-century Athens.

Kathleen Freeman, *Greek City-States* (*Norton). The immense diversity among the poleis is exemplified by detailed examination of nine representative city-states.

## The Zenith and Decline of Classical Greece

All the readings suggested under Chapter 5 are appropriate here, but the political history of the fifth and fourth centuries is best approached through the historical writings of the Greeks themselves:

Herodotus, *The Histories*, trans. by A. de Selincourt (*Penguin).

Thucydides, *The History of the Peloponnesian War*, many translations. We recommend Richard Crawley's (*Modern Library).

Xenophon, *The Persian Expedition*, trans. Rex Warner (*Penguin).

M. I. Finley, ed. and trans., *Greek Historians* (*Viking). Contains much of Herodotus, Thucydides, Xenophon, and Polybius.

Plutarch, *The Rise and Fall of Athens* (*Penguin). Biographies of nine Greeks who determined the course of Greek history around the period of the Peloponnesian War, written by a Roman citizen of the early second century A.D.

F. J. Frost, *Democracy and the Athenians* (*Wiley). Well-chosen selections from ancient and modern writers on aspects of Greek democracy.

## The Hellenic Mind

F. M. Cornford, *Before and After Socrates* (\*Cambridge). A short, lucid account of Greek thought from the Ionians through Aristotle written by a distinguished scholar. Another excellent work by the same author is *From Religion to Philosophy* (\*Harper).

A. H. Armstrong, *An Introduction to Ancient Philosophy* (\*Beacon). An unusually clear survey from the beginnings to St. Augustine.

T. Africa, *Science and the State in Greece and Rome* (\*Wiley). The role of science in relation to the state is freshly interpreted, and brief comparisons are suggested between Mediterranean societies and societies of the Near and Far East.

J. B. Bury, *Ancient Greek Historians* (\*Dover). A scholarly overview of the entire range of Greek historiography from the early epics to the Greek impact on Roman historians.

W. K. C. Guthrie, *Greek Philosophers* (\*Harper). Clear, perceptive, and well written.

Bruno Snell, *The Discovery of the Mind* (\*Harper). A provocative interpretive study tracing the rise of self-awareness in philosophy, literature and the arts.

There are many useful translations from the Greek sources, among which the following are especially recommended:

Willis Barnstone, ed. and trans., *Greek Lyric Poetry*, (\*Bantam). An anthology that ranges from the seventh-century B.C. to the Byzantine Empire.

Hugh Tredennick, ed. and trans., *The Last Days of Socrates* (\*Penguin, rev. ed.). Four dialogues of Plato which cast particular light on the end of Socrates' career.

Scott Buchanan, ed., B. Jowett, trans., *The Portable Plato* (\*Viking).

Benjamin Jowett and Thomas Twining, trans., *Aristotle's Politics and Poetics* (\*Viking).

## The Culture of the Golden Age

H. J. Rose, *Handbook of Greek Literature* (\*Dutton). The most satisfactory survey of this rich subject.

G. M. Richter, *Handbook of Greek Art* (\*Phaidon). The authoritative work on Greek art from the archiac period onward.

V. Ehrenberg, *People of Aristophanes* (\*Shocken). An entertaining and penetrating examination of the characters and society reflected in Aristophanes' plays.

Charles Seltman, *Women in Antiquity* (\*Macmillan). The author argues that women did in fact enjoy much freedom until the advent of Christianity.

H. D. F. Kitto, *Greek Tragedy* (*Anchor). The author has the grace and insight necessary to approach this demanding subject.

W. H. Auden, ed., *The Portable Greek Reader* (*Viking). Perhaps the best of many available anthologies.

L. R. Lind, ed. and trans., *Ten Greek Plays in Contemporary Translations* (*Riverside Editions). All three of the great fifth-century tragedians are represented here. There are numerous other paperback editions of fifth-century plays.

Robert Flacelière, *Daily Life in Greece at the Time of Pericles* (Macmillan). The best work on life in the Golden Age.

## The Hellenistic Age

W. W. Tarn, *Hellenistic Civilisation*, rev. by Tarn and G. T. Griffith (*Meridian). The classical account of the post-Classical age.

Benjamin Farrington, *Greek Science* (*Penguin). A thorough and comprehensive study running from the Ionians to Ptolemy and Galen in the second century A.D.

Ulrich Wilcken, *Alexander the Great* (*Norton). A distinguished biography, scholarly and readable.

Major-General J. F. C. Fuller, *The Generalship of Alexander the Great* (*Minerva). Analyzes the tactics and strategy of Alexander's four great battles.

A. D. Nock, *Conversion* (*Oxford). A keen, thoughtful analysis of religious thought and behavior in Hellenistic and Roman society.

Max Cary, *A History of the Greek World from 323 to 146 B.C.* (2nd ed., Methuen). An excellent, balanced account of Hellenistic history —political, economic, military, intellectual, and cultural.

Marshall Claggett, *Greek Science in Antiquity* (*Collier). A lucid treatment by a major historian of science.

# PART THREE
# ROME

# 11

---

# The Rise of Rome

**Carthage and Magna Graecia** | Had Alexander lived to middle age instead of dying at thirty-two he might well have led his conquering armies westward into Italy, Sicily and North Africa. Here he would have encountered three vigorous cultures: Carthage, the city-states of Magna Graecia, and the rapidly-expanding republic of Rome.

Carthage was originally a Phoenician commercial colony, but its strategic location on the North African coast, just south of Sicily, gave it a stranglehold on the western Mediterranean. It soon developed an extensive commercial empire of its own and far outstripped the Phoenician homeland in power and wealth. Carthage established a number of commercial bases in western Sicily which brought her face-to-face with the Greek city-states that dominated the eastern sections of the island.

The Greek poleis of Sicily and southern Italy, known collectively as Magna Graecia, were products of the age of Greek colonization in the eighth and seventh centuries. Their political evolution ran parallel to that of the city-states in Greece;

they experienced the same violent struggles between aristocratic, oligarchic, and democratic factions and the same intense cultural creativity. And like Old Greece, Magna Graecia
was tormented by intercity warfare. By Alexander's time the
Sicilian polis of Syracuse had long been the leading power of
the area, but the smaller poleis guarded their independence
jealously. Real unification was delayed until the Roman conquests of the third century brought these Greek cities under
the sway of a common master.

**Early Rome** | The rise of Rome from an inconsequential cen-
tral-Italian village to the mastery of the ancient Mediterranean world is perhaps history's supreme success story. The
process was slow as compared with the dazzling imperialistic
careers of Persia and Macedon, but it was far more lasting.
There was nothing meteoric about the serious, hard-headed
Romans—they built slowly and well. Their great military virtue was not tactical brilliance but stubborn endurance; they
lost many battles but from their beginnings to the great days
of the Empire they never lost a war. Since it was they who ultimately provided the ancient world with a viable and all-en-
compassing political framework, students of history have always been fascinated by the development of Roman political
institutions. Rome's greatest contributions were in the realm
of law, government, and imperial organization. In her grasp
of political realities lay the secret of her triumphant career.

The beginnings of Roman history are obscure. It seems
likely that by about 750 B.C. settlers were living in huts on
the Palatine Hill near the Tiber River. Gradually, several
neighboring hills were settled, and around 600 these various
settlements joined together to form the city-state of Rome.

The strategic position of this cluster of hills, fifteen miles
inland on one of Italy's greatest rivers, was of enormous importance to Rome's future growth. Ancient ocean-going ships
could sail up the Tiber to Rome but no farther, while at the
same time Rome was the lowest point at which the river
could be bridged easily. Hence Rome was a key river-crossing

and road junction and also, at least potentially, a seaport. It was at the northern limit of a fertile agricultural district known as Latium whose rustic inhabitants, the Latins, gave their name to the Latin language. Immediately north of Rome lay the district of Etruria (the modern Tuscany) whose highly civilized inhabitants, the Etruscans, shaped the culture of the earliest Romans.

The Etruscan ruling class seems to have migrated to Etruria from Asia Minor around 800 B.C. bringing with it into central Italy important elements of the rich cultural heritage of the eastern Mediterranean and the Near East. The Etruscans borrowed heavily from the Greeks. Their art, their city-state political structure, and their alphabet were all Hellenic in inspiration, but they adapted these cultural ingredients to their own needs and created out of them a vivacious, pleasure-loving civilization of considerable originality.

It was in Etruscan form that Greek civilization made its first impact on Rome. The Romans adopted the Greek alphabet in its Etruscan version and perhaps through Etruscan inspiration they organized themselves into a city-state, thereby gaining an inestimable advantage over the numerous half-civilized tribes in the region between Etruria and Magna Graecia. During much of the sixth century, Rome was ruled by kings of Etruscan background whose talented and aggressive leadership made the Romans an important power among the peoples of Latium. The community grew in strength and wealth, and an impressive temple to the Roman god Jupiter was built in Etruscan style atop one of the hills. Rome was becoming a city in fact as well as in name.

About 509 B.C. the Roman aristocracy succeeded in overthrowing its Etruscan king, transforming Rome from a monarchy into an aristocratic republic. The king was replaced by two magistrates known as consuls who were elected annually by an aristocratic Senate and who governed with its advice. The consuls exercised their authority in the name of the Roman people but in the interests of the upper classes. The governing elite was composed of wealthy landowners known as

patricians who defended their prerogatives zealously against
the encroachments of the lower classes—the plebeians or
plebs. Plebeian-patrician intermarriage was strictly prohibited,
and for a time the plebeians were almost entirely without political rights.

But step by step the plebeians improved their condition
and expanded their role in the government. They began by
organizing themselves into a kind of private corporation
known as the Council of Plebs. They elected representatives
called tribunes to be their spokesmen and represent their interests before the patrician-controlled Roman government.
The tribunes acquired the remarkable power of vetoing, in
the name of the plebeians, measures issuing from any organ
of government. Moreover, anyone violating the sanctity of a
tribune's person was to be punished by death. Under the
leadership of their tribunes the plebeians were able to act as a
unit and to make their strength felt. On at least one occasion
they seceded as a body from the Roman state, leaving the patrician governors with nobody to govern and the patrician
army officers with no troops to lead.

In about 450 B.C. the Romans took the important step of
committing their legal customs to writing. The result was
Rome's first law code—the Twelve Tables. By later standards
these laws were harsh (defaulting debtors, for example, suffered capital punishment or were delivered up for sale a-
broad*), but they had the effect of protecting individual
plebeians from the capricious authority of the patrician consuls. The Twelve Tables are exceedingly significant in Roman
constitutional development, constituting as they do the first
great monument in the evolution of Roman law.

Having gained a measure of legal protection, the plebeians
turned to the problem of land distribution and forced the
government to grant them additional farms out of its own
estates and from the territories of newly-conquered peoples.
In time; resolutions ("plebiscites") passed by the Council of
Plebs came to be accepted as the laws of Rome unless vetoed

---

*Enslavement of Roman citizens for debt was abolished in the 300s.

by the Senate. Intermarriage was now allowed between the two orders, and a law of 367 B.C. opened the consulship itself to plebeians. At the same time, or shortly afterwards, it was stipulated that at least one consul must always be a plebeian. In the years that followed plebeians became eligible for all offices of state. Finally, by a law of 287 B.C., the Council of Plebs won the right to have its plebiscites binding on the entire state without being subject to senatorial veto. This was a most remarkable privilege, comparable to the AFL-CIO legislating for the whole American citizenry.

Nevertheless, the rise of the plebs by no means transformed Rome into an egalitarian democracy. The wealthiest of the Roman citizens continued to control their state through a client-patron system that dated back to Rome's earliest times. Like the bosses in American cities, wealthy Romans took large numbers of poor "clients" under their protection, seeing to their economic and legal needs and receiving political support in return. Through their clients, powerful patrons could exercise indirect yet decisive control of Rome's many assemblies and offices, including the Council of Plebs itself.

Meanwhile, the traditional domination by the patricians had gradually given way to a more subtle domination by a new nobility of wealthy, office-holding plebeian and patrician families. According to Roman custom, a family became "noble" when one of its members was elected as a consul, so once the patricians lost their monopoly on the consulship it became possible for rich, politically-active plebeians to enter the nobility. During the fifth and fourth centuries, moreover, a number of plebeian families had accumulated extensive estates, and some of them began to rival patricians in wealth and political influence. Rich plebeians now became patrons themselves, with numerous clients of their own. More and more, the plebeian tribunes tended to be drawn from wealthy and "noble" families. By 287—when plebiscites acquired the force of law—the old division between patrician and plebeian was no longer important. The new patrician-plebeian nobility had become Rome's ruling class.

The machinery of Roman republican government was complex and changing. It included numerous civic officials with various titles and responsibilities and several different legislative assemblies, the most important of which were the Centuriate Assembly and the Tribal Assembly—an official body patterned after the plebeians' private Council of Plebs. Both the Centuriate and Tribal Assemblies were made up of the entire Roman citizenry, but each had its own distinctive function and organization. Both of them reflected the domination of the wealthy.

The Centuriate Assembly was divided into 193 groups known as "centuries," each with a single vote. These centuries were distributed according to socio-economic class, with the richest classes controlling a majority of the centuries. 98 of the 193 centuries were allotted to citizens of considerable wealth, whereas the masses of citizens without any property whatever (the "proles") were lumped into one century, with one vote. Since the richest centuries voted first, and since balloting ceased as soon as a majority was reached, the lesser classes had no voice at all in the Centuriate Assembly unless the wealthy were in disagreement.

The Tribal Assembly was likewise dominated by the wealthy, though less directly. Its members were organized by districts known as "tribes" (the Roman citizenry had traditionally been divided into tribal groups: originally about 20, later 35). Each tribe had a single vote, and although the tribes consisted largely of poorer citizens, the noble families were able to influence the Tribal Assembly through their clients. Four of the tribes were urban and thirty-one were rural, and the difficulty of coming in from the countryside resulted in the thirty-one rural votes being controlled by the nobility and the clients they brought with them.

The nobility was thus able to manipulate both the Centuriate Assembly and the Tribal Assembly, but its primary instrument of power was the Senate. Originally composed of the heads of important families who acted as advisors to the kings, the Senate in the Republic came to be made up of former holders of civic offices, and the senators therefore constituted an impressive reservoir of political talent and experience. Strictly speaking, the Senate was still merely an advisory body, yet because of the unrivaled prestige of its members its actual power far exceeded that of any other organ in the Roman state. Many wealthy plebeians entered the Senate once the civic offices were opened to their order, taking their places alongside the patricians. Thereafter the Senate came to be dominated by an inner core of patrician-plebeian noble families.

Thus, the new nobility retained in practice the control over Roman politics that in theory belonged to all citizens. Nevertheless, Rome's political realism is well illustrated by the rarity of domestic violence during this long era of sweeping constitutional changes. In the years between the fall of the Etruscan monarchy, around 509 B.C., and the law on plebiscites, in 287 B.C., the plebeians won important political powers without the necessity of a major insurrection. Much Roman blood was spilled on battlefields but relatively little on the city's streets. The willingness to settle internal conflicts by compromise—the ability of the patricians to bend before the winds of social change—preserved in Rome a sense of cohesiveness and a spirit of civic commitment without which her conquests would have been inconceivable.

**The Career Of Conquest** | Civic commitment was a hallmark of the early Roman. Devoted to the numerous gods of city, field, and hearth, he was hard working, respectful of tradition, obedient to civil and military authority, and dedicated to the welfare of the state. The backbone of Old Rome was the small, independent farmer who worked long and hard to raise crops from his fields and remained always vigilant against raids by tribesmen from the surrounding hills. To men such as these life was intensely serious. Their stern sobriety and rustic virtues were exaggerated by Roman moralists looking back nostalgicly from a later and more luxurious age, but there can be little doubt that the tenacious spirit and astonishing military success of early republican Rome owed much to the discipline and steadfastness of these citizen-farmers. As triumph followed triumph, as the booty of war flowed into Rome from far and wide, the character of her citizenry inevitably suffered; one of the great tragic themes of Roman history is the gradual erosion of social morality by wealth and power—and by the gradual expansion of huge slave-operated estates at the expense of the small farmer. But long before this process was complete the empire had been won.

The expulsion of the last Etruscan king in about 509 B.C. was followed by a period of retrenchment during which the Romans fought for their lives against the predatory attacks of neighboring tribes. In time an alliance was formed between Rome and the communities of Latium in which Rome gradually assumed the role of senior partner. Hostile tribes were subdued after long, agonizing effort, and shortly after 400 B.C. the Etruscan cities began to fall, one by one, under Roman control. The Romans were usually generous with the Italian peoples whom they conquered, allowing them a good measure of internal self-government, and were therefore generally successful in retaining their allegiance. In time, if a conquered people proved loyal, they might hope to be granted Roman citizenship. In this generous fashion Rome was able to construct an empire far more cohesive and durable than that of Periclean Athens. (Neither Pericles nor any of his contemporaries could have conceived of granting citizenship to non-Atticans.) Gradually, the Roman conquests gained momentum. Battles were often lost—Rome itself was sacked in 387 B.C. by an army of Gauls from the north—but the Romans brushed off their defeats and pressed on. By 265 B.C. all Italy south of the Po Valley was under their control. Etruscan power had collapsed and even the Italian cities of Magna Graecia acknowledged Roman supremacy. Now, midway through the third century, Rome took her place alongside Carthage and the three great Hellenistic successor states as one of the leading powers of the Mediterranean world.

Carthage and Rome stood face to face, and in 264 B.C. these two great western powers became locked in the first of three savage conflicts known as the Punic Wars (after Poenus, the Latin word for Phoenician or Carthaginian). Rome was now forced to build a navy and take to the sea. The wars, especially the first two, were long and bitter. Rome lost numerous battles, scores of ships, and warriors and seamen by the hundreds of thousands. During the Second Punic War (218–201 B.C.) the armies of the masterly Carthaginian general Hannibal swept back and forth across Italy winning victory after victory, and only the dogged determination of the Romans and the loyalty of their subject-allies saved the state from extinction. But the Romans hung on, suffering many defeats but always managing to win the last battle. At the conclusion of the Third Punic War in 146 B.C. Carthage was in ruins and her far-flung territories in Africa, Sicily, and Spain were in Roman hands.

In the meantime Rome was drawn almost inadvertently into the rivalries among the Hellenistic kingdoms of the eastern Mediterranean. Ptolemaic Egypt, Seleucid Asia, Antigonid Macedon, and the several smaller Greek states had long been at one another's throats; Rome's victories over Carthage increased her power to the point where she was stronger than any one of them. Greek states frequently sought Roman aid against their enemies, and more often than not the Romans gave the requested support to maintain the balance of power in the east and to prevent any one Greek kingdom from becoming dangerously strong. Rome entered the Greek world more as a pacifier than as a conqueror, but eventually she tired of her endless task as referee and remained to rule. During the second century almost all the Hellenistic world fell either directly or indirectly under Roman control. Rome won a decisive victory over the Seleucids in 189 B.C.; she conquered Macedon in 168 B.C.; in 146 she demolished the ancient Peloponnesian city of Corinth and transformed Greece into a Roman province under the direct authority of a governor appointed by the Roman state. The remaining Hellenistic kingdoms were now completely overshadowed and had no choice but to bow to Rome's leadership. Gradually they too became provinces.

Rome followed no blueprint for conquest—indeed many of

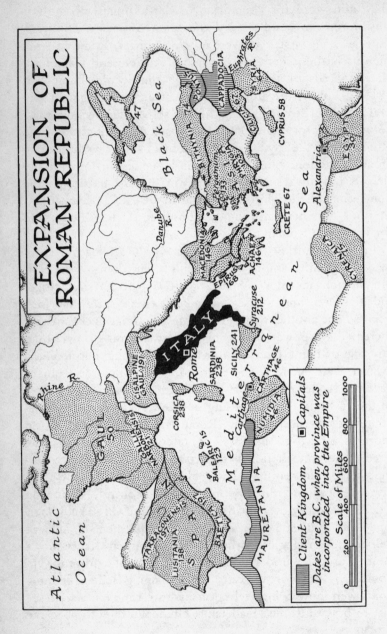

Expansion of the Roman Republic.

her leaders were isolationists who would have preferred to remain aloof from the Greek east—but the political conditions
of the Hellenistic states exerted a magnetic attraction that
proved irresistible. As the second century drew toward its
close Rome was the master of the Mediterranean world.
There now arose the baffling problem of adapting a government designed to rule a city-state to the needs of an empire.

**Social and Political Changes: 264 to 146 B.C.** | The years of
the three Punic Wars witnessed a transformation in the structure and spirit of Rome itself. These changes can be attributed partly to the intoxicating effect of unimagined wealth
and military success that gradually undermined the old civic
virtue and encouraged a mood of arrogance and materialism.
More specifically, as Rome was conquering the Greek world
she was falling increasingly under the influence of Hellenistic
culture. Roman writers such as Cato the Elder lamented that
Roman soldiers were corrupted by the luxuries of eastern
Mediterranean lands. Ultimately, Greece was perhaps the victor after all. The full tide of Hellenistic skepticism and individualism, that had earlier done so much to dissolve the
Greek polis, now began its corrosive work on Roman conservatism and civic dedication. As in Greece, the effects of this
process were both good and bad. What Rome lost in civic virtue she gained in cultural and intellectual depth, for prior to
her Hellenization, Rome was almost totally lacking in high
culture. The Stoic notion of universal brotherhood was a
singularly appropriate philosophy for a great empire, and it
was a fortunate thing for the conquered peoples that in later
years so many Roman statesmen became Stoics. But with
Greek art, literature, and learning came the disquieting Hellenistic feeling of drift and alienation, aggravated by the shift
from family farms to plantations.

Both Carthage and the Hellenistic successor states had emphasized the large plantation over the small independent
farm. Now, as the conquests brought vast wealth and hordes
of slaves into the hands of the Roman upper classes, most of

central and southern Italy was converted into huge farms
known as *latifundia*, worked by slaves and operated according to the latest Carthaginian and Hellenistic techniques of
large-scale scientific farming. Where the small farms had produced grain, the *latifundia* concentrated on the more lucra-
tive production of wine and olive oil or the raising of sheep.
The small farmers, whose energy and devotion had built the
Roman Empire, were subjected to such heavy military demands that they found it increasingly difficult to maintain
their farms. Many sold out to the *latifundia* owners and
flocked into the cities, especially Rome itself, where they
were joined by multitudes of penniless immigrants from the
provinces and transformed into a chronically unemployed,
irresponsible mob. In later years their riots terrorized the government; their hunger and boredom eventually gave rise to
the custom of subsidized food and free entertainment of an
increasingly sadistic sort—"bread and circuses."

While Rome was engaged in her struggle with Carthage, important changes were occurring in the social structure of the
Roman elite. With the acceleration of commerce, a new class
of businessmen and public contractors was developing that in
time acquired such wealth as to rival the landed nobility. This
new class came to be known as the equestrian order because
the wealth of its members enabled them to serve in the Roman army as cavalry rather than infantry. The equestrian
class was effectively excluded from the Senate. Fundamentally apolitical except in instances when their own interests
were at stake, the equestrians were content to share with the
nobility the rising living standards that were coming into
Rome with military triumphs and increased contact with the
Hellenistic world. As the equestrians and landed nobility
came to live in increasing luxury, the gap between rich and
poor steadily widened, and the pressures of social unrest began to threaten the traditional stability of Roman civilization.

Meanwhile the Roman government, which had earlier
acted with restraint toward its subject allies in Italy, was

proving incapable of governing justly its newly acquired overseas territories. Most of Rome's non-Italian holdings were organized as provinces ruled by aristocratic Roman governors
and exploited by Roman tax gatherers. Infected with the selfishness and greed of Hellenistic individualism at its worst,
governor and tax gatherer often worked in partnership to
bleed the provinces for personal advantage. The grossest
kinds of official corruption were tolerated by the Roman
courts of law, whose aristocratic judges hesitated to condemn
dishonest officials of their own class for the sake of oppress-
ed but alien provincials. Indeed, some provincial governors
made it a practice to set aside a portion of their booty to
bribe the courts.

**Violence and Revolutions: the Last Century of the Republic |**
The deep-seated problems that afflicted Rome brought about
a century-long period of violence and unrest, between 133
and 30 B.C., that resulted ultimately in the downfall of the
Republic and the advent of a new imperial government. The
first steps toward revolution were taken by two reform-mind-
ed noblemen, the brothers Tiberius and Gaius Gracchus, who
adovcated a series of popular reform measures and thereby
built up a powerful faction among the Roman commoners
who were struggling against the entrenched aristocracy of
wealth. Tiberius Gracchus served as tribune in 133 B.C. and
Gaius held the same office a decade later. The two Gracchi
were deeply concerned with the ominous course of the Republic. Both recognized that the decline in able recruits for
the Roman army and the deterioration of morale among the
citizenry were caused by the virtual elimination of the small
farm from central Italy. Their solution was to create out of
the vast public lands owned by the Roman state a multitude
of new farms for the dispossessed. This was a courageous and
compassionate program, but the virtuous Roman farmer of
yesteryear could not be conjured back into existence at this
late moment. As it happened, most of the public lands had
long before fallen under the *de facto* control of powerful

noble families. Long accustomed to farming state lands for their own profit, the nobles reacted frigidly to the proposal that they should now give up portions of these lands so that the state might create small farms for the impoverished. In the political holocaust that followed, both Gracchi were murdered—Tiberius in 133, Gaius in 121. The landed nobility demonstrated that, despite past concessions, it was still in control. But it also betrayed its political and moral bankruptcy. Violence had been introduced into Roman political affairs, and the whirlwind now unleashed was to buffet the Republic for a century and finally demolish it.

For a generation the lower classes continued to press for the Gracchan reforms, and the landed nobility found itself pitted not only against the masses but sometimes against the equestrian order as well. But the great political fact of the last republican century was the rise of individual adventurers who sought to use successful military careers as springboards to political power. During the decade of the eighties, two able military commanders, Marius and Sulla, contended against one another for political supremacy. Marius drew much of his support from the lesser classes, whereas Sulla tended to ally with the wealthier and more established, but both were motivated strongly by personal ambition. In 106 B.C. Marius had taken the portentous step of abolishing the property qualification for military service and recruiting volunteers from the poorest classes. Prior to Marius' reform, the resources of Roman military manpower had been declining alarmingly, but now the jobless masses thronged into the legions. Military service became, for many, the avenue to economic security, since soldiers of a successful and politically influential general could often expect to receive upon retirement a gift of land from the Senate. The army began to acquire a more professional outlook than before, and soldiers came to identify themselves with their commanders rather than with the state. The opportunities for a ruthless and ambitious general with a loyal army at his back were limitless. But Marius was unwilling to go so far as to seize and overthrow the government.

The more ruthless Sulla had no such scruples. In 83 B.C. he marched on Rome with his own devoted legions and, in the following year, made himself dictator. Once in power, he purged his enemies and proscribed a number of wealthy citizens, enriching himself from their confiscated fortunes. But Sulla had no intention of holding power indefinitely. A conservative at heart, he employed his dictatorial prerogatives to establish a series of laws that confirmed and strengthened the power of the inept Senate, then retired to affluent private life on his country estate in Campania, leaving the Republic to stagger on.

In the decade of the sixties, the great senatorial orator Cicero strove desperately to unite senators and equestrians against the growing threat of the generals and the riotous urban masses. Cicero's consummate mastery of Latin style, both in his orations and in his writings, earned him a lofty position in the field of Roman literature, but his political talents proved inadequate to the task of saving the Republic. His dream of reconciling the interests of senators and equestrians was shattered by the selfishness of each, and his efforts to perpetuate the traditional supremacy of the Senate were doomed by the Senate's own incapacity, by the smoldering unrest of the city mobs, and by the ambition of the military commanders. It was Cicero's misfortune to be a conservative in an epoch of revolutionary turbulence—a statesman in an age of generals.

The Republic was now approaching its final days in an atmosphere of chaos and naked force. The dominant political figures of Cicero's generation were military commanders such as Pompey and Julius Caesar who bid against one another for the backing of the lower classes, seeking to convert mob support into political supremacy. Characteristically, the three great men of their age, Pompey, Cicero, and Caesar, all met violent deaths. The failure of republican government was now manifest, and the entire imperial structure seemed on the verge of collapse. As it turned out, however, Rome was to emerge from her crisis transformed and strengthened, and her empire was to endure for another five-hundred years. The salvation of the Roman state out of the wreckage of the old order constitutes one of antiquity's most stunning achievements. To this transformation we now turn.

## CHRONOLOGY OF THE ROMAN REPUBLIC

All Dates B.C.

| | |
|---|---|
| 753: | Traditional date for Rome's founding |
| c.616–509: | Etruscan kings rule Rome |
| c.450: | Twelve Tables |
| 367: | Plebeians eligible for consulship |
| 287: | Loss of Senate's veto power over plebiscites |
| 265: | Rome controls all Italy south of the Po |
| 264–241: | First Punic War |
| 218–201: | Second Punic War |
| 149–146: | Third Punic War |
| 146: | Macedonia becomes Roman province |
| 133: | Tribunate of Tiberius Gracchus |
| 123–122: | Tribunate of Gaius Gracchus |
| 121: | Gaius Gracchus killed |
| 106: | Marius reorganizes military recruitment |
| 83–80: | Sulla re-establishes republican constitution |
| 60–44: | Caesar a dominant force in Roman politics |
| 43: | Cicero killed |

# 12

## The Principate

**Julius Caesar and Augustus** | The new order, which saved Rome from the agonies of the late Republic and brought a long era of peace and stability to the Mediterranean world, was chiefly the handiwork of two men: Julius Caesar and his grandnephew, Augustus. Julius Caesar was a man of many talents—a superb general, a brilliant and realistic politician, and a distinguished man of letters whose lucid and forthright *Commentaries on the Gallic Wars* was a significant contribution to the great literary surge of the late Republic. Above all, Caesar was a man of reason who could probe to the core of any problem, work out a logical, practical solution, and then carry his plan to realization.

Caesar managed to ride the whirlwind of violence and ruthless ambition that was shattering Roman society during the mid-first century B.C. His political intuition and unswerving faith in himself and his stars catapulted him to increasingly important political and military offices during the turbulent sixties. Opposed and distrusted by the conservative Senate, he allied himself with Pompey, a talented, disgruntled gen-

eral, and Crassus, an ambitious millionaire. These three formed an extralegal coalition of political bosses, known to later
historians as the "First Triumvirate," which succeeded in
dominating the Roman state.

Leaving Italy in the hands of his two colleagues, Caesar
spent most of the following decade (58–50 B.C.) in Gaul
leading his army on a spectacular series of campaigns that
resulted in the conquest of what is now France and Belgium
and established his reputation as one of history's consummate military scientists. Caesar's conquest of Gaul pushed the
influence of Rome far northward from the Mediterranean
into the heartland of western Europe. The historical consequences of his victories are immense, for in the centuries that
followed, Gaul was thoroughly Romanized. The Roman influence survived the later barbarian invasions to give medieval
and modern France a romance tongue and to provide western
Europe with an enduring Greco-Roman cultural heritage.

While Caesar was winning his triumphs in Gaul his interests
in Italy were suffering. His advocacy of land redistribution
and of other policies dear to the hearts of the lower classes
earned him the hostility of the Senate, and his spectacular
military success threatened to thwart Pompey's own ambition to be first among Romans. Out of their common fear of
Caesar, Pompey and the Senate now joined forces, and in 49
B.C. Caesar was declared a public enemy. His career at stake,
Caesar defied the Roman constitution by leading his own
loyal army into Italy. In a series of dazzling campaigns during
49 and 48 B.C., he defeated Pompey and the hostile members
of the Senate. Pompey fled to Egypt and was murdered
there, and the Senate had no choice but to come to terms
with the man who now towered unchallenged over Rome.

Caesar was a magnanimous victor. He restored his senatorial opponents to their former positions and ordered the exe-
cution of Pompey's murderer. He could afford to be generous
for he was now the unquestioned master of the state. The Republic had traditionally, in time of grave crisis, concentrated
all power in the hands of a dictator who was permitted to ex-

ercise his virtually unlimited jurisdiction for six months only. Caesar assumed the office of dictator and held it year after year. Ultimately he forced the Senate to grant him the dictatorship for life. He also assumed the key republican office of consul and retained the title of *pontifex maximus* (supreme pontiff or chief priest of the civic religion) which he had held for some years. In 44 B.C. he received the unprecedented honor of having a temple dedicated to his "genius" (his family spirit), and the month of July was named in his honor. The political institutions of the Republic survived but they were now under his thumb. He controlled the appointment of civic officials, manipulated the assemblies, and overawed the Senate. The whole Roman electorate had become his clients.

Caesar used his power to reform the Republic along logical, realistic lines. The magnitude of his reforms defies description. He introduced a radically new calendar that, with one minor adjustment, is in almost universal use today. He organized numerous distant colonies that drained off a considerable number of Rome's unemployed masses, and halved the Roman bread dole. He did much to reform and rationalize Italian and provincial government and to purge the republican administration of its abuses. In short, he was the model of what would much later be called an "enlightened despot." Some historians have supposed that Caesar was aiming at a monarchy along Hellenistic lines, but it is more accurate to view him as a supremely talented Roman applying his intellect to the rational solution of Roman problems.

Caesar's remarkable success attests to the creative power of the human mind; his ultimate failure, however, suggests that in human affairs reason is not always enough—that the ingrained historical traditions of a people will resist the surgery of even the most skillful rationalist reformer. Caesar's reforms were immensely beneficial to the people of the Empire, but he went too far too fast. His disregard for republican institutions was too cavalier, and his assumption of the dictatorship for life alarmed powerful elements in the Senate. On the Ides of March (March 15), 44 B.C., he was stabbed to death at a Senate meeting by a group of conservative senatorial conspirators led by Brutus and Cassius. As they rushed from the Senate the assassins shouted, "Tyranny is dead!" They were wrong: it was the Republic that was dead, and Rome now had only the choice between one-man rule and anarchy. By killing Caesar, they had given up the former for the latter.

Caesar's assassination resulted in fourteen more years of civil strife during which the conservative party of Brutus and Cassius struggled against would-be heirs to Caesar's power while the heirs struggled against one another. In the complex maneuvers of this civil war some of the most famous figures in ancient history played out their roles. Mark Antony, Caesar's trusted lieutenant, defeated Brutus and Cassius in battle, and both committed suicide. The golden tongued Cicero, Rome's supreme literary craftsman, was murdered for his hostility to Antony. And when the fortunes of war turned against them, Antony and his exotic wife, Queen Cleopatra of Egypt, took their own lives.

The ultimate victor in these struggles was a young man who had been virtually unknown at the time of Caesar's death. Octavian, the later Augustus, Caesar's grandnephew and adopted son, had woven his way through the era of strife with matchless skill. A young man of eighteen when Caesar died, Octavian proved to the world that he was in truth Caesar's heir. For although inferior to Caesar in generalship and perhaps also in sheer intellectual strength, Octavian was Caesar's superior as a realistic, practical politican. During his long, illustrious reign Octavian completed the transformation of the Roman state from Republic to Empire. But his reforms were more traditionalist in appearance than Caesar's, and he succeeded—where Caesar had failed—in winning the Senate's respect. He reformed the Romans and made them accept it.

**The Augustan Age** | In 31 B.C. Octavian's forces crushed those of Antony and Cleopatra at Actium. A year later Octavian entered Alexandria as master of the Mediterranean world. He was then the same age as Alexander at the time of his death, and it might be supposed that the two world-conquerors, both young, brilliant, and handsome, had much in common. But Octavian refused to visit Alexander's tomb in Alexandria, observing, so it was said, that true greatness lies not in conquest but in reconstruction. It is appropriate, therefore, that Octavian's immense historical reputation lies not in his military victories but in his accomplishments as peacemaker and architect of the Roman Empire.

The reformation of Rome, completed by Octavian, gave the Mediterranean world two centuries of almost uninterrupted peace and prosperity during which classical culture developed and spread to the outermost reaches of the Empire. This unprecedented achievement caused men, in the turbulent centuries that followed, to look back longingly at the almost legendary epoch of the "Roman Peace." Octavian accomplished the seemingly impossible task of reconciling the need for one-man rule with the republican traditions of Old Rome. He preserved the Senate; indeed, increased its prestige. He retained the elected republican magistracies. He made no attempt to revive the office of dictator, for he preferred to manipulate the government in more subtle ways. He controlled the army and, like Caesar, he concentrated various key republican offices in his own person. Eventually he went beyond Caesar himself in being granted the power of a tribune (including the right to initiate legislation and the unlimited right of veto, which tribunes had originally exercised in behalf of the plebeian order). With its great flexibility, the tribunician power was ideal for Augustus's needs and became the single most important instrument of imperial control. Future emperors dated their reigns from their receipt of it.

In 27 B.C. Octavian was given the novel name of Augustus, a term that carried with it no specific power but had a connotation of reverence—almost holiness. And like Caesar he arranged to have a month (August) named in his honor. But much as he may have enjoyed these distinctions, he took pains to maintain a relatively modest public image. He commonly used the simple title of *princeps* ("first citizen"), which conveyed the suggestion that he was the leading Roman—nothing more. He lived fairly modestly, associated freely with his fellow citizens, revered the dignity of the Senate, and dressed and ate simply. It has been said that the Principate (the government of the *princeps*) was the exact opposite of the government of modern England: the former a monarchy masquerading as a republic, the latter a republic masquerading as a monarchy. But if the Principate was at heart a monarchy, it was by no means an arbitrary one. Augustus ruled with a keen sensitivity toward popular and senatorial opinion and a respect for tradition. Ancient Rome, like modern England, had no paper constitution, but it had a venerable body of political customs—an unwritten constitution—that Augustus treated with cautious deference.

Still, Augustus was the true master of Rome. The nature of the Empire was such that the liberty of the old Republic simply could not be preserved. The Roman electorate was incapable of governing the Empire, and a democratic Empire with universal suffrage was inconceivable. Roman liberty was the single great casualty of the Principate, but its loss was rendered almost painless by the political deftness of the first *princeps*. In its place Augustus provided peace, security, prosperity, and justice. The administration of the provinces was now closely regulated by the *princeps* and the corruption and exploitation of the late Republic were reduced. In Rome itself an efficient imperial bureaucracy developed that was responsible to the *princeps* alone. Although class distinction remained strong, it was now possible for an able man from one of the lesser orders to rise in the government service. And Augustus sought out and supported men with literary and artistic gifts as a matter of policy.

The stable new regime, the promise of enduring peace, the policy of "careers open to talents," and the leadership of Augustus himself combined to evoke a surge of optimism, patriotism, and creative originality. In the field of arts and letters the "Augustan Age" is the climax of Roman creative genius, surpassing even the literary brilliance of the troubled late Republic of which Cicero stands as the supreme example. Under Augustus, Roman artists and poets achieved a powerful synthesis of Greek and Roman elements. Roman architecture was obviously modeled on the Greek, but it just as obviously expressed a distinctively Roman spirit. Roman temples rose higher than those of classical Greece and conveyed a feeling that was less serene—more imposing and dynamic; less horizontal—more vertical. Augustan poetry—the urbane and faultless lyrics of Horace, the worldly, erotic verses of Ovid, the majestic cadences of Virgil—employed Greek models and ideas in original and characteristically Roman ways. Rome's supreme poem, Virgil's *Aeneid*, was cast in the epic form of Homer and dealt, as Homer's *Odyssey* did, with the voyage of an important figure in the Trojan War. But Aeneas, Virgil's hero, was also the legendary founder of Rome, and the poem is shot through with patriotic prophecies regarding the great destiny of the state which Aeneas was to found. Indeed, some readers have seen in Aeneas a symbol of Augustus himself. The *Aeneid* conveys the feeling of hope—that the Roman people, founded by Aeneas and now led by the great peacemaker Augustus, have at last fulfilled their mission to bring enduring concord and justice to the tormented world:

> But Rome! 'tis thine alone, with awful sway,
> To rule mankind, and make the world obey,
> Disposing peace and war thy own majestic way;
> To tame the proud, the fetter'd slave to free:
> These are imperial arts, and worthy thee.*

**Imperial Leadership After Augustus** | Augustus died at the age of 76 in A.D. 14. During the decades following his death the Principate grew steadily more centralized and more efficient. The imperial bureaucracy expanded, the provinces were reasonably well governed, taxes were relatively light and

*Aeneid*, Book VI (tr. John Dryden—very loosely).

The Pantheon, Rome, A.D. 118 to 125 (*Alimari—Art Reference Bureau*).

intelligently assesed, the law became increasingly humane, and the far-flung inhabitants of the Empire enjoyed unprecedented peace and prosperity. It is a tribute to Augustus' wisdom that the system which he created was sturdy enough to endure and flourish despite the relative incapacity of many of his imperial successors.

The abilities of the first-century emperors ranged from uninspired competence to downright madness, descending on occasion to the vain-glorious absurdity of a Nero or the grotesque lunacy of a Caligula who wallowed in the pleasure of watching his prisoners being tortured to death. Caligula is reported to have allowed his favorite horse to dine at the imperial table during formal state dinners, consuming the finest food and wines from jeweled dishes and goblets. At Caligula's death he was on the point of raising the beast to the office of consul. Caligula and Nero were autocrats of the worst type, and both were removed violently from power. On the whole, however, the emperors of the early Principate retained the traditional "constitutional" attitudes exemplified by Augustus himself.

The second century A.D. witnessed a dramatic improvement in the quality of imperial leadership. Rome's rulers between A.D. 96 and 180 have been called the "five good emperors." One nineteenth-century historian described them in these enthusiastic words: "For eighty-four years a series of sovereigns, the best, the wisest and the most statesmanlike that the world has ever seen—Nerva, Trajan, Hadrian, Antoninus, Marcus Aurelius—sat upon the throne of the world."* And although more recent historians would look askance at such sweeping praise, there can be no question but that the "five good emperors" were sovereigns of uncommon ability.

The high level of imperial leadership that characterized this era can be attributed largely to the temporary solving of one of the knottiest dilemmas in the whole imperial system—the problem of succession. In theory the Senate chose the *prin-*

*Thomas Hodgkin, *The Dynasty of Theodosius* (Oxford, 1889), p. 18.

*ceps,* but in fact the succession usually fell to a close relative
of the previous emperor and was often arranged by the emperor in advance. Too often this hereditary principle allowed
the Empire to fall into the hands of an unworthy ruler; occasionally a disputed succession was settled by violence and
even civil war. But none of the great second-century emperors—Trajan, Hadrian, Antoninus Pius, or Marcus Aurelius—
came to power by normal hereditary succession. In each case,
the previous emperor *adopted* as his son and successor a
younger man of outstanding ability. The policy of adoption
worked well for a time, but it did not represent a deliberate
rejection of the hereditary succession principle. It was simply
a consequence of the fact that none of the "five good emperors" had a son except Marcus Aurelius—the last of them. Marcus followed the hereditary principle—which had never con-
sciously been abandoned—and chose his own son, the incompetent Commodus, as his heir. With the disastrous reign of
Commodus (A.D. 180–192) the great age of imperial rule
came to an end. It was followed by a century of military des-
potism, assassinations, economic and administrative breakdown, cultural decay, and civil strife which almost brought
an end to the Roman state.

**The Empire Under The Principate** | Before moving into the
troubled third century, let us look briefly at the condition of
the Empire at its height. During the two centuries from the
rise of Augustus to the death of Marcus Aurelius (31 B.C.–
A.D. 180), the Empire expanded gradually to include a vast
area encircling the Mediterranean Sea. It extended from the
Euphrates to the Atlantic—from the Sahara to the Danube,
the Rhine, and the Cheviot Hills of northern Britian. A considerable amount of territory was added to the Empire under
Augustus, and several later emperors, notably Trajan, made impressive conquests. But most of the emperors were content to
guard the frontiers and preserve what had earlier been won.

The burden of defending the far-flung frontiers rested on
an army of some 300,000 to 500,000 men, organized on

principles laid down by Augustus. Infantry legions manned by Roman citizens on long-term enlistments were supplemented by auxiliary forces, both infantry and light cavalry, made up of non-Romans who were granted citizenship at the end of their extended terms of service. The army was concentrated along the frontiers except for the small, privileged praetorian guard that served the emperor in Rome itself. A high degree of mobility was insured by the superb system of roads which connected the city of Rome with her most remote provinces. Paved with stones fitted closely together, and running in straight lines mile after mile, these roads were nearly as eternal as the city they served. They eased the flow of commerce as well as the movement of troops and remained in use many centuries after the Roman Peace was shattered by anarchy and Germanic invasions.

The Empire's greatest commercial artery was not built of stone; it was the Mediterranean, completely surrounded by imperial territory and referred to affectionately by the Romans as *Mare Nostrum*—"our sea." Roman fleets patrolled the Mediterranean and kept it free of pirates for the first time in antiquity so that peaceful shipping could move unimpeded between the many ports of the Empire. Now as never before the immense territories encompassed by the Roman frontiers were well governed, well policed, and bound together by roads and protected seaways.

Under the aegis of the Roman Peace, commercial prosperity, Roman institutions, and classical culture spread far and wide across the Empire. As distant provinces became increasingly Romanized the meaning of the words "Rome" and "Roman" gradually changed. By the time of Augustus these terms were no longer confined to the imperial city and its inhabitants but had come to embrace the greater part of Italy. Now, as the decades of the Roman Peace followed one another, citizenship was progressively extended to more and more provincials until finally, in A.D. 212, every free inhabitant of the Empire was made a citizen. By then, the emperors themselves often came from the provinces: the great second-

The Roman Empire at its

## THE ROMAN EMPIRE AT ITS HEIGHT EARLY 2ND CENTURY

Roman Empire

Areas temporarily under the influence of the Roman Empire

S A R M A T I A

Caspian Sea

DACIA
(107–275 A.D.)

Danube R.

MOESIA

Black Sea

CAUCASUS MTS.

THRACE

Byzantium

BITHYNIA

PONTUS

ARMENIA
(115–117 A.D.)

PARTHIAN EMPIRE

EDONIA

GALATIA

CAPPADOCIA

ASIA

Pergamum

Aegean
Sea

Smyrna

Ephesus

MESOPOTAMIA
(115–117 A.D.)

Athens

PAMPHYLIA

CILICIA

Tarsus

Tigris R.

Sparta

LYCIA

Antioch

RHODES

SYRIA

Euphrates R.

CRETE

CYPRUS

Tyre

Damascus

ean        Sea

Jerusalem

Alexandria

ARABIA

CYRENAICA

E G Y P T

ARABIA

Syene

height, early second century.

century emperor Trajan, for example, was a native of Spain. In time the terms "Rome" and "Roman" acquired a universal connotation: a Greek monarch in Constantinople, a Frankish monarch at Aachen, a Saxon monarch in Germany, a Hapsburg in Vienna could, in later centuries, all refer to themselves as "Roman emperors."

The most conspicuous effect of Romanization was the spread of cities across the entire Empire. The city-state, the characteristic political unit of the Greco-Roman world, now extended to the outermost provinces—to Gaul, Spain, the lands along the Rhine and Danube, even remote Britain. The city still retained much local self-government and normally controlled the rural territories in its vicinity. In other words, the city was the key unit of local administration, the government of the Roman state remained fundamentally urban. Paradoxically, the cities of the Empire, especially in the West, were of relatively minor importance as commercial and manufacturing centers. Rome experienced no industrial revolution and, although small-scale urban industry often flourished, particularly in the East, the economy of the Empire remained fundamentally agrarian. Many of the western cities, including Rome itself, consumed far more than they produced. Unlike the cities of medieval and modern Europe they were not economically self-sufficient but acted as parasites on the imperial economy. Basically they were administrative and military centers whose mercantile significance was secondary. During the first two centuries of the Empire the economy was prosperous enough to support them, but this would not always be the case. In time the cities would decline, and with them the whole political structure of the Greco-Roman world.

In the early Empire, as in the late Republic, slaves played a crucial role in the economy, especially in agriculture. But as the frontiers gradually ceased to expand and the flow of war captives diminished, the chief source of slaves was cut off. Large landholders now began to lease major portions of their estates to free sharecroppers called *coloni,* who tended to fall

more and more under the control of their landlords and sank
slowly to a semiservile status akin to that of the medieval
serfs. The *coloni*, like the impoverished masses who continued to crowd the larger cities, enjoyed little of the buoyant
prosperity of the Principate. The age of the "five good emperors" was, by ancient standards, an epoch of material well-
being, but it would be absurd to compare it to the abundance
of the advanced industrial states of today. Roman society always included, beneath its veneer, a vast, wretched substra-
tum of half-starved peasants and paupers.

The condition of the lower classes would have been still
worse but for the humane policies of the imperial government. It was particularly among the great second-century emperors that Stoic attitudes of human brotherhood, compassion, and social and political responsibility took hold. Unlike
Caligula and Nero, who used their power to indulge their bizarre whims, emperors such as Hadrian and Marcus Aurelius
viewed their own authority as a trust; a responsibility to govern in the interests of the people whether rich or poor. The
Empire of the second century is ornamented by its social
conscience no less than by its leadership in military and administrative affairs.

**The Silver Age** | The cultural epoch from approximately the
death of Augustus to the death of Marcus Aurelius is known
as the Silver Age. Less illustrious than the golden Augustan
Age, it nevertheless produced literary, intellectual, and artistic accomplishments of the first order. Some observers have
seen in Silver Age writers such as the Stoic Seneca, the satirist
Lucian, and the essayist Pliny the Younger a decline in creative genius. They have stressed the pretentious, ornate style
of second-century literature, the stale conformity of second-
century art. And they have attributed these shortcomings to
the "homogenization" of imperial society and the dullness of
peace and security. Such judgments are necessarily relative,
and many sensitive spirits through the centuries have viewed
writers of the Silver Age with enormous admiration. What-

ever one may think of the originality and excellence of Silver
Age literature, there can be no question but that culture and
learning spread outward and downward. Remote provincial
cities built temples and baths, theaters and triumphal arches
in the Roman style. Libraries and schools were scattered
abundantly across the Empire, and the extent of urban literacy is demonstrated by the many irreverent and obscene
scribblings and campaign slogans discovered by modern exca-
vators on the buildings of Pompeii, buried and preserved by
the eruption of Vesuvius in A.D. 79.

Alexandria, the Hellenistic metropolis, retained its commercial and intellectual importance throughout the age of the
Principate, producing some of the most brilliant early Christian theologians as well as several distinguished scientists who
developed and synthesized the achievements of earlier Hellenistic science. Greek and Hellenistic astronomical thought, for
example, was developed into a sophisticated and comprehensive model of the universe by Ptolemy of Alexandria (d.
about A.D. 180) who expanded the work of his predecessors
into a geocentric world-system that accounted, with remarkable precision, for the observed motions of the sun, moon,
and planets among the stars. Ptolemy also wrote the most
complete geography of antiquity, and Galen (A.D. 131 to
201), a great medical scientist from Hellenistic Pergamum,
produced a series of works on biology and medicine that
dominated these fields for more than a thousand years. The
*Meditations* of Marcus Aurelius, the last of the "five good
emperors," is a moving expression of the Stoic philosophy
that deepened and humanized so much of the best thought of
the era. In literature and art, science and philosophy, the Silver Age produced an effortless synthesis of Greek and Roman
traditions. The rich legacies of Greece, Rome, and the ancient
Orient were summarized and fused.

**Roman Law** | Of all the achievements of this epoch perhaps
the most far reaching—certainly the most distinctively Roman—was the development of imperial law. The rigid code of

the Twelve Tables was gradually broadened and humanized by the magistrates of the later Republic and early Empire, by the great legists of the second and third centuries A.D., and by the enlightened intervention of the emperors themselves. As the Romans became acquainted with more and more peoples, each with its unique set of laws and customs, they gradually emancipated themselves from the peculiarities of their own law and strove to replace it by a body of fundamental principles drawn from the laws of all people. The *Jus Gentium* or "law of peoples" slowly transformed the Roman code into a legal system suitable to a vast, heterogeneous empire.

The evolution of Roman law into a universal system of jurisprudence owed something also to the Greek concept of the *Jus Naturale*—the "law of nature"—which has played a prominent role in the history of Western thought. More abstract than the *Jus Gentium*, the "law of nature" or "natural law" is based on the belief that in a divinely ordered world there are certain universal norms of human behavior which all people tend to follow, regardless of their own individual customs and traditions. These norms, based on general principles of political and social justice, served to rationalize and humanize the law of the Empire and to provide it with a sturdy philosophical foundation. Accordingly, Roman law, a product of the Latin practical political genius influenced by Greek speculative thought, gave substance to the Augustan ideal of justice. Codified at enormous effort by the sixth-century emperor Justinian, it has become a crucial part of the Western heritage—the basis of many legal systems to this day in Europe and her former colonies.

# 13

## The Spiritual Metamorphosis

**Roman Religion** | Roman religion is immensely complex, for the Romans not only recognized many gods but had numerous separate cults. Like the Greek city-states, Rome had its official civic deities—Jupiter and Juno, Minerva and Mars, and many others, who by the later Republic had become identified with parallel gods of the Greek Olympic religion. The Roman Jupiter was the Greek Zeus, the Roman Minerva was the Greek Athena, and so on. Besides these Roman state deities there were the innumerable local gods of the cities and districts of the Empire. And in Rome itself as well as throughout the Empire there were countless unofficial cults that normally enjoyed the toleration of the Roman state. None of these pagan cults was exclusive; none claimed a monopoly on truth, and a single individual might without compromise participate in several of them.

With the coming of the Principate an important new element was added to the state religion: the cult of the emperor. Both Augustus and his successors (with a few notorious exceptions) were deified by the Senate after their deaths. In those provinces where god-kings were traditional the *princeps* was viewed as a deity while still alive, and it soon became customary for Romans and provincials alike to participate in formal religious observances to the deified emperors as well as to the major deities of the city of Rome. These observances were at heart more patriotic than religious. They were useful in encouraging the allegiance of diverse peoples and, in accordance with religious attitudes of the day, few objected to the addition of a handful of new deities to the divine crowd that they already worshiped. To the Jews, and later the Christians, these religio-patriotic observances were another matter, for the jealous God of the Jews permitted the worship of no other. But Rome recognized the Jews as a people apart and usually excused them from participation in the official cults. The Christians, on the other hand, suffered gravely from their refusal to worship the emperors and gods of Rome. To the Romans such intransigence savored of both atheism and treason. It is no accident that Christianity alone of all the religions of the Empire was the object of serious Roman persecution.

**The Mystery Cults** | The centuries after Augustus witnessed a slow but fundamental shift in Roman religious attitudes, from the veneration of the traditional gods of household, clan, and city to the worship of transcendental deities imported from the Near East. The gods of Old Rome, like those of the Greek Olympus, had safeguarded the welfare of social and political groups; the new gods cared little for such things but offered instead the hope of individual redemption, salvation, and eternal life. As the Roman imperial age progressed, the allegiance of the people slowly shifted from Jupiter and Minerva to the Egyptian Isis, the Persian Mithras, the Phrygian Great Mother, the Syrian sun god, and other exotic deities who offered solace and eternal joy to people for whom the world—even the world of the Roman Peace—was not enough.

This surge of mysticism was actually a continuation and

expansion of a trend we have already observed among the Hellenistic Greeks. The same forces that had encouraged widespread rootlessness and disorientation in the Hellenistic world were now at work throughout the Roman Empire: cosmopolitanism, gradually-increasing autocracy, and, among the underprivileged masses, grinding poverty and loss of hope. The shift from civic god to savior god, from this world to the next, constitutes a profound transformation in mood— a repudiation of traditional Greco-Roman humanism. As the peace of the second century gave way to the anarchy of the third, the high hopes of classical humanism—the dream of a rational universe, an ideal republic, a good life—were beginning to seem like cruel illusions, and the movement toward the mystery cults gained enormous momentum.

**Neo-Platonism** | The older pagan cults were by no means completely supplanted, but they were altered by the growth of otherworldliness that accompanied the third-century anarchy. This trend toward a transcendental outlook is especially conspicuous in the leading philosophical movement of the century, Neo-Platonism. The philosopher Plotinus, one of the deepest and subtlest minds of the age, popularized the doctrine of a single god, infinite and beyond reason, unknowable and unapproachable except through an ecstatic trance. Plotinus taught that God was the source of reality and existence. All being, both physical and spiritual, radiated outward from him like concentric ripples in a pool. Greek rationalism was an empty thing indeed for those who believed that the only truth worth knowing lay outside the scope of human reason.

In the later Empire all that was vital in pagan religion was incorporated into a spacious Neo-Platonic synthesis. The Neo-Platonists taught that the gods of the pagan cults were all symbols of the one unknowable god and that each pagan cult therefore had validity. Paganism became increasingly monotheistic: Zeus, Jupiter, Mithras, were simply different aspects of a single transcendent deity. In this atmosphere the distinction between the traditional pagan cults and the mys-

tery religions faded. By the fourth century Greek rationalism
and humanism had been superseded almost entirely by a
spirit of otherworldliness, divine revelation, and yearning for
eternal life. Neo-Platonic philosophy and Near Eastern religion were accompanied by astrology, magic, charlatanism,
and other practices which had never been absent from Greco-
Roman society but which now dominated popular thinking
as never before. It was in this supernatural environment that
Christianity won its decisive victory.

**The Emergence of Christianity** | Two fundamental trends
characterized religious development in the Roman Empire:
the growing impulse toward mysticism that we have just ex-
amined, and the interpenetration and fusion of doctrines and
practices between one cult and another—a process known as
*syncretism*. The syncretic quality of Christianity itself has
often been observed, for in numerous instances its beliefs and
rituals were similar to those of earlier religions. Obviously,
Christianity drew heavily from Judaism—nearly all the earliest Christians were Jews—but it was also anticipated in various particulars by Zoroastrianism, Mithraism, the Isis-Osiris
cult, the Greek mysteries of Dionysus and Demeter, and even
Stoicism. Many Christian doctrines had long pre-Christian
histories: the concept of death and resurrection, the sacramental meal, baptism, personal salvation, and the brotherhood of man under the fatherhood of God, to name but a
few. Yet Christianity was far more than a new configuration
of old ideas, and it would be misleading to think of it as
merely another of the oriental mystery religions. It differed
from them above all in two basic ways: (1) its god was the
jealous God of the Hebrews, unique in all antiquity in his
claims to exclusiveness and omnipotence, and now released
by Christianity from his association with a specific chosen
people and universalized as the God of all mankind; (2)
Christianity's founder and Savior was a vivid historic personality, Jesus, beside whom such mythical idealizations as
Mithras or Isis must have seemed tepid and diffuse.

Jesus, a younger contemporary of Augustus, was a figure in the Hebrew prophetic tradition whose life and teachings show little, if any, Greek influence. He is depicted in the Gospels as a warm, magnetic leader who miraculously healed the sick, raised the dead, and stilled the winds. His miracles were seen as credentials of the divine authority with which he claimed to speak. His ministry was chiefly to the poor and outcast, and in Christianity's early decades it was these classes that accepted the faith most readily. He preached a doctrine of love, compassion, and humility; like the prophets he scorned empty formalism in religion and stressed the simple life of generosity toward both friend and enemy and devotion to God. He does not seem to have objected to ritual as such, but only to ritual infected with pride and complacency and divorced from love and kindness. In the end, he was condemned for subversion and crucified, as a result of his severe criticisms of the established Jewish priesthoods, combined apparently with his claim to speak with divine authority and the nervousness of Roman officials who feared a religion-inspired national uprising.

According to the Gospels, Jesus's greatest miracle was his resurrection—his return to life three days after he died on the cross. He is said to have remained on earth for a short period thereafter, giving solace and inspiration to his disciples, and then to have "ascended" into heaven with the promise that he would return in glory to judge all souls and bring the world to an end. The first generations of Christians expected this second coming to occur quickly, and it is perhaps for that reason among others that formal organization was not stressed in the primitive Church.

The early Christians not only accepted Christ's ethical precepts but worshiped Christ himself as the divine incarnation of the omnipotent God. The Christ of the Gospels distinguishes repeatedly between himself—"the Son of Man"—and God—"the Father"—but he also makes the statement, "I and the Father are one," and he enjoins his disciples to baptize all persons "in the name of the Father and the Son and the Holy Spirit." Hence, Christianity became committed to the difficult and sophisticated notion of a triune Godhead with Christ as the "Son" or "Second Person" in a Trinity that was nevertheless one God. The doctrine of the Trinity gave Christianity the unique advantage of a single infinite, philosophically respectable god who could be worshiped and adored in the person of the charismatic, lovable, tragic Jesus. The Christian deity was both transcendent and concrete.

**The Early Church** | The first generation of Christianity witnessed the beginning of a deeply significant development whereby the Judeo-Christian heritage was modified and enriched through contact with the main currents of Greco-Roman culture. Christ's own apostles were no more influenced by Hellenism than their master, and some of them sought to keep Christianity strictly within the ritualistic framework of Judaism. But St. Paul, a Hellenized Jew and early convert—and a Roman citizen—succeeded in steering the Church toward his own vision of a universal brotherhood. Christians were to be free of the strict Jewish dietary laws and the requirement of circumcision (which were bound to discourage the conversion of non-Jews). Christianity would be open to all people everywhere who would accept Jesus as God and Savior—and open also to the bracing winds of Hellenistic thought. St. Paul traveled far and wide across the Empire preaching the message of Christ as he interpreted it, winning converts, and establishing Christian communities in many towns and cities of the Mediterranean world. Other Christian missionaries, among them St. Peter and his fellow apostles who had been Christ's immediate followers, devoted their lives as St. Paul did to traveling, preaching, and organizing—often at the cost of ridicule and persecution. Tradition has it that St. Paul and all the apostles died as martyrs. Their work was tremendously fruitful, for by the end of the apostolic generation Christianity had become a ponderable force among the underprivileged masses of Italy and the East. Within another century it had spread throughout the greater part of the Empire.

From the first, the Christians regularly engaged in a sacra-

mental meal which came to be called the "eucharist" or
"holy communion" and was viewed as an indispensable chan-
nel of divine grace through which the Christian was infused
with the spirit of Christ. By means of another important sac-
rament, baptism, the postulant was initiated into the brotherhood of the Church, had all sins forgiven, and received the
grace of the Holy Spirit. A person could be baptized only
once, and baptized persons alone could consider themselves
true Christians. But in the early Church baptism was often
delayed until adulthood and therefore many unbaptized persons were associated with the Christian communities without
being Christians in the full sense of the word.

As Christian historical documents became more common,
in the second and third centuries A.D., the organization of
the Church begins to emerge more sharply than before. The
documents of this period disclose an important distinction
between the clergy, who govern the church and administer
the sacraments, and the laymen, who play a more passive
role. The clergy itself was divided into several ranks: the most
important were the bishops, who served as rulers and pastors
over the various urban communities, and the priests, who led
the services and administered the sacraments under a bishop's
jurisdiction. Moreover, the bishops themselves were of various degrees of eminence. Above the common bishops were
the metropolitans or archbishops who resided in cities of special importance and exercised control over an extensive surrounding area. At the top of the hierarchy were the bishops
of the three or four greatest cities of the Empire—Rome,
Alexandria, Antioch, and later Constantinople. These great
leaders were known as patriarchs and exercised spiritual authority (often more theoretical than real) over vast areas of
the Mediterranean world. As time went on, the bishop of
Rome—the pope—came to be regarded more and more as the
foremost of the patriarchs, but the actual establishment of
papal authority over even the Western Church was to require
the efforts of many centuries.

**Christianity And Hellenism** | Medieval and modern Christian theology is a product of both the Hebrew and the Greek traditions. The synthesis of these two intellectual worlds began not among the Christians but among the Jews themselves, especially those who had migrated in large numbers to Alexandria. Here Jewish scholars—in particular a religious philosopher of the early first century A.D. named Philo Judaeus—worked toward the reconciliation of Jewish revelation and Greek philosophy. Drawing heavily from Aristotle, the Stoics, and particularly Plato, they developed a symbolic interpretation of the Old Testament that was to influence Christian thought enormously over the centuries.

Following many of the fruitful leads of Philo Judaeus, Christian theologians strove to demonstrate that their religion was more than merely an appealing myth—that it could hold its own in the highest intellectual circles. The Savior Christ, for example, as true God and true man, constituted a unique synthesis of the material and spiritual worlds. In Greek terms, Christ reconciled Plato's dualism, for Christ was at once a particular person and an archetype. Christianity differed from most of the Near-Eastern mystery religions—especially those emanating from Persia—in its refusal to reject the material world. Matter could not be evil of itself, for it was the handiwork of God; the human body could not be wholly corrupt, for Christ himself was a human in the fullest physical sense. Christianity was therefore not so radically at odds with Greek humanism as, say, Mithraism—although its concept of sin and its doctrine of the fall of man through the disobedience of Adam were obviously far removed from the traditional humanistic point of view of the Greeks.

The fusion of matter and spirit, so fundamental to orthodox Christianity, did not escape challenge among the early Christians. Once the expectation of an immediate second coming began to fade, many Christians started to examine their faith more philosophically than before and to raise difficult questions about the nature of Christ and the Trinity. A diversity of opinions emerged, some of which seemed so inconsistent with the majority view that they were condemned as heresies. As questions were raised and orthodox solutions agreed upon, the Christian faith became increasingly specific and elaborate.

The early heresies sought to simplify the nature of Christ and the Trinity. One group, known as the Gnostics, interpreted Christ in the light of the Persian notion that matter was evil. They insisted that Christ was not really human but only a divine phantom—that a good God could not degrade himself by assuming a physical body. Others maintained that Christ was not fully divine—not an equal member of the triune Godhead. The latter position was taken up by the fourth-century Arians whom we will meet in the next chapter. The orthodox position lay midway between these two views: Christ was fully human and fully divine—a coequal member of the Holy Trinity who had always existed and always would, but who was incarnate in human form at a particular moment in time, and who walked the earth, taught, suffered, and died, as the man Jesus. Thus the synthesis of matter and spirit was strictly preserved, and Christ remained the bridge between the two worlds.

The Christian apologists—the defenders of orthodoxy against pagan attacks from without and heterodox attacks from within—played a crucial role in formulating and elaborating Christian doctrine, coping with problems that had not even occurred to the apostolic generation. It is of the highest significance that a great many serious Christian intellectuals worked within the framework of the Greek philosophical tradition. This is especially true of the greatest of them, the Alexandrian theologian Origen (d. 254), who created a coherent, all-inclusive Christian philosophical system on Platonic foundations. Origen was one of the foremost thinkers of his age and is widely regarded as one of the supreme minds in the entire history of the Church. His religious system did not win over the pagan intellectual world at a blow—indeed, several of his conclusions were rejected by later Christian orthodoxy—

but he and other Christian theologians succeeded in making Christianity meaningful and intellectually attractive to men whose thinking was cast in the Greco-Roman philosophical mold. The greatest of the Greek philosophers, so these Christian writers said, had been led toward truth by the inspiration of the Christian God.

**Christianity And The Empire** | At the very time that Christian theology was being Hellenized, pagan thought itself was shifting increasingly toward otherworldliness. Origen's greatest pagan contemporary was the Neo-Platonist Plotinus. Indeed, the two may have studied under the same teacher. The growth of a transcendental outlook throughout the ancient world created an atmosphere highly nourishing to a salvation religion such as Christianity. The Christian viewpoint was becoming increasingly in tune with the times; it appealed to an age hungry for a consoling doctrine of personal redemption. Yet its triumph was by no means assured, for it faced other salvation religions such as Mithraism and the Isis cult—and traditional Greco-Roman paganism in its new, otherworldly, Neo-Platonic guise. Against these rivals Christianity could offer the immense appeal of the historic Jesus, the growing profundity of its theology, the infinite majesty of its God, and the compassion and universalism of its message preserved and dramatized in its canonical books—the Old and New Testaments. Few social groups were immune to its attraction. The poor, humble, and underprivileged made up the bulk of its early converts, and it was to them that Jesus had directed much of his message. Intellectuals were drawn by its Hellenized theology, men of feeling by its mysticism, and men of affairs by the ever-increasing effectiveness of its administrative hierarchy. For in administration no less than in theology the Church was learning from the Greco-Roman world.

Before the collapse of the Roman Empire in the West, Christianity had absorbed and turned to its own purposes much of Rome's heritage in political organization and law, carrying on the Roman administrative and legal tradition into

the medieval and modern world. Roman civil law was paralleled by the canon law of the Church. The secular leadership
of the Roman Empire gave way to the spiritual leadership of
the Roman pope, who assumed the old republican and imperial title of *pontifex maximus*—supreme pontiff—and preserved much of the imperial ceremonial of the later Empire.
As imperial governors and local officials gradually disappeared in the West, their traditions were carried on, in a new spiritual dimension, by metropolitans and bishops. Indeed, the
*diocese*, the traditional unit of a bishop's jurisdiction, was
originally an imperial administrative district. In this organizational sense, the medieval Church has been described as a
ghost of the Roman Empire. Yet it was far more than that,
for the Church reached its people as Rome never had, giving
the impoverished masses a sense of participation and involvement that the Empire had failed to provide.

From the beginning the Christians of the Empire were a
people apart—convinced that they alone possessed the truth
and that 'the truth would one day triumph, eager to win new
converts to their faith, uncompromising in their rejection of
all other religions, willing to learn from the pagan world but
unwilling ever to submit to it. They angered their pagan contemporaries by their cohesiveness (which doubtless appeared
to outsiders as clannishness), their sense of destiny, and their
refusal to worship the state gods. As a consequence, Christians were often objects of suspicion, hatred, and persecution. The emperors themselves followed a rather inconsistent
policy toward them. Violent persecutions, such as those
under Nero and Marcus Aurelius, alternated with long periods
of inaction. On the whole, the Church throve on the blood of
its martyrs; the persecutions were neither sufficiently ruthless
nor sufficiently lengthy to come near wiping out the entire
Christian community. The pagan emperors could have learned much from the Christian inquisitors of sixteenth-century
Spain on the subject of liquidating troublesome religious
minorities.

Most of the emperors, if they persecuted Christians at all,

did so reluctantly. The "good emperor" Trajan instructed a provincial governor neither to seek Christians out nor to heed anonymous accusations. (Such a procedure, Trajan observed, is inconsistent with "the spirit of the age.") A person was to be punished only if he should be denounced as a Christian, tried, and found guilty, and then persist in his refusal to worship the imperial gods. One can admire the Christian who would face death rather than worship false gods, but one can also sympathize with emperors such as Trajan who hesitated to apply their traditional policy of religious toleration to a people who seemed bent on subverting the Empire.

The persecutions of the first and second centuries, although occasionally severe, tended to be limited in scope to specific local areas. The great empire-wide persecutions of the third and early fourth centuries were products of the crisis that Roman civilization was then undergoing. The greatest imperial persecution—and the last—occurred at the opening of the fourth century under the Emperor Diocletian. By then Christianity was too strong to be destroyed, and the failure of Diocletian's persecution must have made it evident that the Empire had no choice but to accommodate itself to the Church. A decade after the outbreak of this last persecution, Constantine, the first Christian emperor, undertook a dramatic reversal of religious policy. Thereafter the Empire endorsed Christianity rather than fighting it, and by the close of the fourth century the majority of the inhabitants of the Empire had been brought into the Christian fold. Rome and Jerusalem had come to terms at last.

# 14

---

# The Dominate

**The Third Century** | The turbulent third century—the era of Origen and Plotinus—brought catastrophic changes to the Roman Empire. The age of the "five good emperors" (A.D. 96–180) was followed by a hundred troubled years during which anarchy alternated with military despotism. The army, now fully conscious of its strength, made and unmade emperors. One military group fought against another for control of the imperial title—a man might be a general one day, emperor the next, and dead the third. No less than nineteen emperors reigned during the calamitous half-century between 235 and 285, not to mention innumerable usurpers and pretenders whose plots and machinations contributed to the general chaos. In this fifty-year period every emperor save one died violently—either by assassination or in battle. The Silver Age had given way to what one contemporary historian describes as an age "of iron and rust."

A crucial factor in the chaos of the third century was the problem of the imperial succession. And all too often the problem was solved by force alone. As the power of the army increased and military rebellions became commonplace, the imperial succession came more and more to depend on the whim of the troops. Perhaps the most successful emperor of the period, Septimius Severus (193-211), maintained his power by expanding and pampering the army, opening its highest offices to every class, and broadening its recruitment. A military career was now the logical avenue to high civil office, and the bureaucracy began to display an increasingly military cast of mind. The old ideals of Republic and Principate were less and less meaningful to the new governing class, many of whom rose from the dregs of society through successful army careers to positions of high political responsibility. These new administrators were often men of strength and ability, but they were not the sort who could be expected to understand the Old Roman political traditions. As emperors like Septimius Severus increased taxes to fatten their treasuries and appease their troops, the civilian population was becoming powerless and impoverished. Septimius's dying words to his sons are characteristic of his reign and his times: "Enrich the soldiers and scorn the world."

Rome's troubles in the third century cannot be ascribed entirely to the drift toward military absolutism. As early as the reign of Marcus Aurelius (161-180) the Empire had been struck by a devastating plague that lingered on for a generation and by an ominous irruption of Germanic tribesmen who spilled across the Rhine-Danube frontier as far as Italy itself. Marcus Aurelius, the philosopher-emperor, was obliged to spend the greater part of his reign campaigning against the invaders, and it was only at enormous effort that he was able to drive them out of the Empire. During the third century the Germans attacked with renewed fury, penetrating the frontiers time and again, forcing the cities to erect protective walls, and threatening for a time to destroy the Empire. And the Germanic onslaught was accompanied by furious attacks from the east by the recently reconstituted Persian Empire led by able kings of its new Sassanid dynasty.

Rome's crucial problems, however, were internal ones.

During the third century, political disintegration was accompanied by social and economic breakdown. The ever-rising fiscal demands of the mushrooming bureaucracy and the insatiable army placed an intolerable burden on the inhabitants of town and country alike. Peasants fled from their fields to escape the tax collector, and the urban middle classes became shrunken and demoralized. The self-governing town, the bedrock of imperial administration and, indeed, of Greco-Roman civilization itself, was beginning to experience serious financial difficulties, and as one city after another turned to the emperor for financial aid, civic autonomy declined. These problems arose partly from the parasitical nature of many of the Roman cities, partly from rising imperial taxes, and partly from the economic stagnation that was slowly gripping the Empire. Long before the death of Marcus Aurelius, Rome had abandoned her career of conquest in favor of a defensive policy of consolidation. The flow of booty from conquered lands had ceased, and the Empire as a whole was thrown back on its own resources and forced to become economically self-sufficient. For a while all seemed well, but as administrative and military expenses mounted without a corresponding growth in commerce and industry, the imperial economy began to suffer. The army, once a source of riches from conquered lands, was now an unproductive encumbrance.

By the third century, if not before, the Roman economy was shrinking. Plagues, hunger, and a sense of hopelessness resulted in a gradual decline in population. At the very time when imperial expenses and imperial taxes were rising, the tax base was contracting. Prosperity gave way to depression and desperation, and the flight of peasants from their farms was accompanied by the flight of the savagely-taxed middle classes from their cities. The Empire was now clogged with beggars and brigands, and those who remained at their jobs were taxed all the more heavily. It was the western half of the Empire that suffered most. What industry there was had always been centered in the East, and money was gradually flowing eastward to productive centers in Syria and Asia

Minor and beyond to pay for luxury goods, some of which came from outside the Empire altogether—from Persia, India, and China. In short, the Empire as a whole, and the western Empire especially, suffered from an unfavorable balance of trade that resulted in a steady reduction in Rome's supply of precious metals.

The increasingly desperate financial circumstances of the third-century Empire forced the emperors to experiment in the devaluation of coinage, adulterating the precious metals in their coins with baser metals. This policy provided only temporary relief. In the long run it resulted in runaway inflation that further undermined the economy and contributed to the destruction of the commercial class. Between A.D. 256 and 280 the cost of living rose 1000 percent.

The third-century anarchy reached its climax during the 260s. By then the Roman economy was virtually in ruins. Germanic armies were rampaging across the frontiers. Gaul and Britain in the West and a large district in the East had broken loose from imperial control and were pursuing independent courses. The population was speedily shrinking, and countless cities were in an advanced state of decay. Rome's demise seemed imminent.

As it turned out, however, the Empire was saved by the tremendous efforts of a series of stern leaders who rose to power in the later third century. The Roman state survived in the West for another two centuries and in the East for more than a millennium. But the agonies of the third century left an indelible mark on the reformed Empire. The new imperial structure which brought order out of chaos was profoundly different from the government of the Principate: it was an autocracy no longer disguised by republican trappings.

**The Reforms Of Diocletian** | Even at the height of the anarchy there were emperors who strove desperately to defend the Roman state. After A.D. 268 a series of able, rough-hewn emperor-generals from the Danubian provinces managed to turn the tide. They restored the frontiers, smashed the invading Germanic and Persian armies, and recovered the alienated provinces in Gaul and the East. At the same time measures were undertaken to arrest the social and economic decay that was debiliting the Empire. These policies were expanded and brought to fruition by Diocletian (284–305) and Constantine (306–337), to whom belong the credit—and responsibility—for reconstituting the Empire along authoritarian lines. No longer merely a *princeps*, the emperor was now *dominus et deus*—lord and god—and it is therefore appropriate that the new regime that replaced the Principate should be called the "Dominate."

In the days of Augustus it had been necessary, so as not to offend republican sensibilities, to disguise the power of the emperor. In Diocletian's day the imperial title had for so long been dishonored and abused that it was necessary to exalt it. Diocletian and his successors glorified the office in every way imaginable. The emperor became a remote, unapproachable figure clothed in magnificent garments, a diadem upon his head. An elaborate court ceremonial was introduced, similar to that of Persia, which included the custom of prostration in the emperor's sacred presence.

Diocletian's most immediate task was to bring to a close the turbulent era of short-lived "barracks emperors" and military usurpers. In order to stabilize the succession and share the ever-growing burden of governing the Empire, he decreed that there would thenceforth be two emperors—one in the East, the other in the West—who would work together harmoniously for the welfare and defense of the state. Each of the two would be known by the title *Augustus*, and each would adopt a younger colleague—with the title *Caesar*—to share his rule and ultimately to succeed him. The Empire was now reorganized into four administrative regions, each supervised by an Augustus or a Caesar. Well aware of the increasing importance of the eastern over the western half of the Empire, Diocletian made his capital in the East and did not set foot in Rome until the close of his reign. A usurper would now, presumably, be faced with the task of overcoming four widely-scattered personages instead of one. The chances of military usurpation were further reduced by Diocletian's rigorous separation of civil and military authority. The army was considerably enlarged, chiefly by the incorporation of Germanic forces who now assumed much of the burden of guarding the frontiers. But it was organized in such a way that the emperor (or emperors) could control it far more effectively than before.

Imperial control was the keynote of this new regime. The Senate was now merely ornamental, and the emperor ruled through his obedient and ever-expanding bureaucracy—issuing edict after edict to regulate and systematize the state. The shortage of money was circumvented by a new land tax to be collected in kind, and the widespread flight from productive labor was reduced by new laws freezing peasants, artisans, and businessmen to their jobs. A vast hereditary caste system quickly developed; sons were required by law to take up the careers and tax burdens of their fathers. Peasants were bound to the land, city dwellers to their urban professions. Workers in the mines and quarries were literally branded. The caste system was more theoretical than real, for these measures were difficult to enforce and a degree of social mobility remained. Nevertheless, the Dominate was a relatively regimented society. Economic collapse was averted, but at the cost of strict social controls. The once-autonomous cities now lay under the hand of the imperial government, and commitment to the Empire was waning among the tax-ridden middle classes, who had formerly been among its most enthusiastic supporters.

But it was Diocletian's mission to save the Empire whatever the cost, and it may well be that authoritarian measures were the only ones possible under the circumstances. For every problem Diocletian offered a solution—often heavyhanded, but a solution nevertheless. A thoroughgoing currency reform had retarded inflation but had not stopped it altogether, so Diocletian issued an edict fixing the prices of most commodities by law. To the growing challenge of Christianity

Diocletian responded, regretfully, by inaugurating a persecution of unprecedented severity. As it turned out, neither the
imperial price controls nor the imperial persecution achieved
their purposes. But the very fact that they were attempted
illustrates the lengths to which the emperor would go in his
effort to hold together the Roman state.

The division of imperial authority among the two Augusti
and the two adopted Caesars was a bold, imaginative attempt
at political reform. Yet it worked effectively only so long as
Diocletian himself was in command. Once his hand was removed, a struggle for power brought renewed civil strife. The
principle of adoption, which the sonless Diocletian had re-
vived without serious difficulty, was challenged by the sons
of his successors. The era of chaos ran from the end of Diocletian's reign in 305 to the victory of Constantine in 312 at
the battle of the Milvian Bridge.

**The Reign of Constantine (306–337)** | Constantine's triumph
in 312 marked the return of political stability and the con-
summation of Diocletian's economic and political reforms.
Diocletian's policy of freezing occupations and making them
hereditary was carried still further by Constantine in an edict
of A.D. 332. Imperial ceremonial was elaborated and imperial
authority grew. In certain respects, however, Constantine's
policies took radical new directions. In place of the abortive
principle of adoption, Constantine founded an imperial dynasty of his own. For a time he was obliged to share authority
with an imperial colleague, but in 324, Constantine defeated
his co-emperor in battle and thereafter ruled alone. Nevertheless, the joint rule of an eastern and a western emperor became common in the years after Constantine's death, and he
himself contributed to the division of the Empire by building
the magnificent eastern capital of Constantinople on the site
of the ancient Greek colony of Byzantium.

Constantinople was a second Rome. It had its own Senate,
its own imposing temples, palaces, and public buildings, and
its own hungry proletariat fed by the bread dole and diverted

by chariot races in its enormous Hippodrome. A few decades after its foundation it even acquired its own Christian patriarch. Constantine plundered the Greco-Roman world of its artistic treasures to adorn his new city and lavished his vast resources on its construction. Founded in A.D. 330, Constantinople was to remain the capital of the Eastern Empire for well over a thousand years, impregnable behind its great walls, protected on three sides by the sea, perpetually renewing its economy through its control of the rich commerce flowing between the Black Sea and the Mediterranean. The age-long survival of the Eastern Empire owes much to the superb strategic location of its capital.

Even more momentous than the building of Constantinople was Constantine's conversion to Christianity and his reversal of imperial policy toward the Church. Although he put off baptism until his dying moments, Constantine had been committed to Christianity ever since his victory at the Milvian Bridge in 312. From that time onward he issued a continuous series of pro-Christian edicts insuring full toleration, legalizing bequests to the Church (which accumulated prodigiously over the subsequent centuries), and granting a variety of other privileges. Christianity was now an official religion of the Empire. It was not yet *the* official religion, but it would become so before the fourth century ended.

Various explanations have been offered for Constantine's conversion. He has been portrayed as an irreligious political schemer bent on harnessing the vitality of the Church to the failing state. But there seems no reason to doubt that in fact his conversion was sincere, if superficial. By the fourth century the Empire's mood was deeply religious and it would therefore be unwise to impose on Constantine the mental framework of a modern skeptic.

**The Christian Empire** | The respite gained by Diocletian's reforms and the subsequent conversion of Constantine made it possible for the Church to develop rapidly under the benevolent protection of the Empire. The years between Constantine's victory in 312 and the final suppression of the Western Empire in 476 were momentous ones in the evolution of Christianity. For one thing, the fourth century witnessed mass conversions to the Christian fold. Perhaps ten percent of the inhabitants of the Western Empire were Christians in 312 (in the East the figure would be considerably higher), whereas by the century's end the now respectable Christians were in the majority. But, as is so often the case, triumph evoked internal dissension, and the fourth century witnessed a violent struggle between orthodoxy and heresy. Here, too, the Christian emperors played a determining role, and it was with strong imperial support that the greatest of the fourth-century heresies, Arianism, was at length suppressed within the Empire.

The Arians maintained that the purity of Christian monotheism was compromised by the orthodox doctrine of the Trinity. Their solution to this conflict was the doctrine that God the Father was the only true god—that Christ the Son was not fully divine. The orthodox Trinitarians regarded this doctrine as subversive to one of their most fundamental beliefs: the equality and codivinity of Father, Son, and Holy Spirit. Constantine sought to heal the Arian-Trinitarian dispute by summoning an ecumenical (universal) council of Christian bishops at Nicaea in A.D. 325. He had no strong convictions himself, but the advocates of the Trinitarian position managed to win his support. With imperial backing, a strongly anti-Arian creed was adopted almost unanimously. The three divine Persons of the Trinity were declared equal: Jesus Christ was "of one substance with the Father."

But Constantine was no theologian. In after years he vacillated, sometimes favoring Arians, sometimes condemning them, and the same ambiguity characterized imperial policy throughout the greater part of the fourth century. Indeed, one of Constantine's fourth-century successors, Julian "the Apostate," reverted to paganism. At length, however, the uncompromisingly orthodox Theodosius I came to the throne (378–395) and broke the power of the Arians by condemn-

ing and proscribing them. It was under Theodosius and his
successors that Christianity became the one legal religion of
the Empire. Paganism itself was banned and persecuted and
quickly disappeared as an organized force.

Orthodox Christianity now dominated the Empire, but its
triumph, won with the aid of political force, was far from
complete. For one thing, the mass conversions of the fourth
century tended to be superficial—even nominal. Conversion
to Christianity was the path of least resistance, and the new
converts were on the whole a far cry from the earlier society of saints and martyrs. It was at this time that many ardent Christians, discontented with mere membership in a respectable, work-a-day Church, began taking to the desert as
hermits or flocking into monastic communities.

Moreover, the imperial program of enforced orthodoxy
proved difficult to carry out. Old heresies lingered on and vigorous new ones arose in the fifth century and thereafter.
Even Arianism survived, not among the citizens of the Empire, but among the Germanic tribes across its frontiers. Beginning around the mid-fourth century, at a time when Arianism was still strong in the Empire, large numbers of Germanic
peoples had been converted to Christianity in its Arian form,
and the Trinitarian policies of Theodosius I had no effect on
them whatever. Accordingly, when the Germanic tribes later
formed their kingdoms on the ruins of the Western Empire,
most of them were separated from their Old-Roman subjects
not only by language and custom but by a deep religious
chasm as well.

Finally, by accepting imperial support against paganism
and heresy, the Church sacrificed much of its earlier independence. The Christians of Constantine's day were so over-
whelmed by the emperor's conversion that they tended to
glorify him excessively. As a Christian, Constantine could no
longer claim divinity, but contemporary Christian writers
such as the historian Eusebius allowed him a status that was
almost godly. To Eusebius and his contemporaries, Constantine was the thirteenth apostle; his office was commissioned
by God; he was above the Church. His commanding position

in ecclesiastical affairs is illustrated by his domination of the
Council of Nicaea, and the ups and downs of Arianism in the
following decades depended largely on the whims of his successors. In the East, this glorification of the imperial office
ripened into the doctrine known as *caesaropapism*—that the
emperor is the real master of both Church and state, that he
is both Caesar and pope—and caesaropapism remained a dominant theme in the Eastern or Byzantine Empire throughout
its long history. Church and state tended to merge under the
sacred authority of the emperor. Indeed, the Christianization
and sanctification of the imperial office were potent forces in
winning for the eastern emperors the allegiance and commitment of the masses of their Christian subjects. Religious loyalty to the Christian emperor provided indispensable nourish-
ment to the East Roman state over the ensuing centuries.
Conversely, widespread hostility toward imperial orthodoxy
in districts dominated by heretical groups resulted in the
alienation and eventual loss to the Byzantine Empire of several of its fairest provinces.

Caesaropapism was far less influential in the West, for as
the fifth century dawned the Western Empire was visibly failing. Western churchmen were beginning to realize that Christian civilization was not irrevocably bound to the fortunes of
Rome. Gradually the Western Church began to assert its independence of state control—with the result that Church and
state in medieval Western Europe were never fused but remained always in a state of tension.

In the era of the Christian Empire the culture of Greco-
Roman antiquity was all but transformed. The sense of otherworldliness, which had long been gaining momentum, produced profound changes in literature and art. Rome drifted
far from the classical Greek culture that it inherited—with its
sturdy, straightforward, superbly-proportioned architecture,
its deeply human drama, its bold flights into uncharted regions of rational thought, and its tensely-controlled, natural-
istic sculpture. Greek classicism had undergone important
modifications in the Hellenistic Age and again during the

Principate. Now, in the late Empire, the otherworldly mood
brought a momentous transmutation of the classical spirit.

There had always been a potent spiritual-mystical element
in Greco-Roman culture, coexisting with the traditional classical concern with the earthly and concrete. Now the mystical element grew far stronger. More and more of the better
minds turned to religious symbolism, spiritual fulfillment,
and individual salvation. Artists were less interested in portraying physical perfection and more interested in portraying
the inner person. The new Christian art depicted slender,
heavily robed figures with solemn faces and deep eyes—win-
dows into the soul. Techniques of perspective, which the
artists of antiquity had developed to a fine degree, mattered
less to the artists of the late Empire. Deemphasizing physical
realism, they adorned their figures with rich, dazzling colors
that stimulated in the beholder a sense of heavenly radiance
and religious solemnity. Majestic churches now began to rise,
their interiors decorated with glistening mosaics portraying
saints and statesmen, Christ and the Virgin, on backgrounds
of blue or gold. Here was an art vastly different from that of
Greek antiquity, with different techniques and different
goals, yet just as successful as the art of the Athenian golden
age, and more fundamentally original than anything the Roman Empire had done before.

**The Doctors of the Latin Church** | During the later fourth
and early fifth centuries, at a time when the Christianization
of the Roman state was far advanced but before the Western
Empire had lost all its vitality, the long-developing synthesis
of Judeo-Christian and Greco-Roman culture reached its climax in the West with the writings of three gifted scholar-
saints: Ambrose, Jerome, and Augustine. These men are regarded as "Doctors of the Latin Church," for their writings
dominated medieval thought. Each of the three was thoroughly trained in the Greco-Roman intellectual tradition;
each devoted his learning and his life to the service of Christianity; each was at once an intellectual and a man of affairs.

Ambrose (about 340–397) was bishop of Milan, which by the later fourth century had replaced Rome as the western imperial capital. He was famed for his eloquence and administrative skill, for his vigor in defending Trinitarian orthodoxy against Arianism, and for the ease and mastery with which he adapted the literary traditions of Cicero and Virgil and the philosophy of Plato to his own Christian purposes. Above all, he was the first churchman to assert that in the realm of morality the emperor himself is accountable to the Christian priesthood. When the powerful Emperor Theodosius I massacred the inhabitants of rebellious Thessalonica, Ambrose barred him from the church of Milan until he had formally and publicly repented. Ambrose's bold stand and Theodosius' submission constituted a stunning setback for the principle of caesaropapism and a prelude to the long struggle between Church and state in the Christian West.

Jerome (about 340–420) was a masterly scholar and a restless, inquisitive reformer with a touch of acid in his personality. He once remarked to an opponent, "You have the will to lie, good sir, but not the skill to lie." Wandering far and wide through the Empire, he founded a monastery in Bethlehem where he set his monks to work copying manuscripts, thereby instituting a custom that throughout the Middle Ages preserved the tradition of Latin letters and transmitted it to the modern world. Like other Christian intellectuals he feared that his love of pagan literature might dilute his Christian fervor, and he tells of a dream in which Jesus banished him from heaven with the words, "Thou art a Ciceronian, not a Christian." But in the end he managed to reconcile pagan culture and Christian faith by using the former only in the service of the latter. His greatest contribution to Christian thought was in the field of biblical translation and commentary—above all, in his scholarly translation of the Scriptures from Hebrew and Greek into Latin. Jerome's Latin Vulgate Bible has been used ever since by Roman Catholics and has served as the basis of innumerable translations into modern languages. It was an achievement of incalculable significance to Western Civilization.

The most profound of the Latin Doctors was Augustine
(354–430) who spent his final forty years as bishop of the
North African city of Hippo. Like Jerome, Augustine worried
about the dangers of pagan culture to the Christian soul. He
finally concluded, much as Jerome did, that Greco-Roman
learning, although not to be enjoyed for its own sake, might
properly be used to elucidate the Faith. Augustine was the
chief architect of medieval theology. Even more than his contemporaries he succeeded in fusing Christian doctrine with
Greek thought—especially the philosophy of Plato and the
Neo-Platonists. It has been said that Augustine baptized
Plato. As a Platonist he stressed the importance of ideas or
archetypes over tangible things, but instead of locating his
archetypes in the abstract Platonic "heaven" he placed them
in the mind of God. The human mind had access to the
archetypes through an act of God which Augustine called
"divine illumination."

As a bishop, Augustine was occupied with the day to day
cares of his diocese and his flock. His contribution to religious thought arises not from the dispassionate working-out
of an abstract system of theology but rather from his responses to the burning issues of the moment. His thought is a fascinating mixture of profundity and immediacy—of the abstract and the human. His *Confessions*, the first psychologic-
ally-sensitive autobiography ever written, tells of his own
spiritual journey through various pagan and heretical cults to
Christian orthodoxy. Implicit in this great book is the hope
that others as misguided as he once was might also be led by
God's grace to the truth in Christ.

Against the several heretical doctrines that threatened
Christian orthodoxy in his day, Augustine wrote clearly and
persuasively on the nature of the Trinity, the problem of evil
in a world created by God, the special character of the Christian priesthood, and the nature of free will and predestination. His most influential work, the *City of God*, was prompted by a sack of Rome by the Visigoths in A.D. 410, which
the pagans ascribed to Rome's desertion of her old gods. Augustine responded by developing a Christian theory of history

which interpreted human development not in political or economic terms but in moral terms. As the first Christian philosopher of history, Augustine drew heavily on the historical in-
sights of the ancient Hebrews. Like the Hebrew prophets of
old, he asserted that kingdoms and empires rose and fell according to a divine plan, but he insisted that this plan lay forever beyond human comprehension. Augustine rejected the
theory, common in antiquity, that history was an endless series of cycles, arguing on the contrary that history was moving
toward a divinely appointed goal. This linear view of history
set something of a precedent for the modern secular concept
of historical progress.

Augustine also rejected the Hebrew notion of tribal salvation, putting in its place the Christian notion of *individual*
salvation. The ultimate units of history were not tribes and
empires but individual, immortal souls. The salvation of
souls, Augustine stated, depends not on the fortunes of
Rome but on the grace of God. Christ is not dependent on
Caesar. And if we look at history from the moral standpoint
—from the standpoint of souls—we see not the clash of armies
or the rivalry of states but a more fundamental struggle between good and evil which has raged through history and
which rages even now within each soul.

Humanity is divided into two classes: those who live in
God's grace and those who do not. The former belong to
what Augustine called the "City of God," the latter to the
"Earthly City." The members of the two cities are hopelessly
intermixed in this world, but they will be separated at death
by eternal salvation or damnation. It is from this transcendental standpoint, Augustine believed, that the Christian
must view history. Only God could know what effect Rome's
decline would have on the City of God. Perhaps the effect
would be beneficial, perhaps even irrelevant.

Augustine is one of the two or three seminal minds in
Christian history. His Christian Platonism governed medieval
theology down into the twelfth century and remains influential in Christian thought today. His emphasis on the special

sacramental power of Christian priests remains a keystone of Catholic theology. His emphasis on divine grace and predestination, although softened considerably by the medieval Church, re-emerged in the sixteenth century to dominate early Protestant doctrine. And his theory of the two cities, although often in simplified form, had an enormous influence on Western historical and political thought over the next millennium.

Ambrose, Jerome, and Augustine were at once synthesizers and innovators. The last great minds of the Western Empire, they operated at a level of intellectual sophistication that the Christian West would not reach again for seven hundred years. The strength of the classical tradition that underlies medieval Christianity and Western Civilization owes much to the fact that these men, and others like them, found it possible to be both Christians and Ciceronians.

# 15

## The Waning of
## the Western Empire

**"Decline and Fall"** | The catastrophe of Rome's decline and fall has always fascinated historians, for it involves not only the collapse of mankind's most impressive and enduring universal state but also the demise of Greco-Roman Civilization itself. The reasons are far too complex to be explained satisfactorily by any single cause—Christianity, disease, slavery, soil-exhaustion, lead-poisoning, or any of the other "master-keys" that have been proposed from time to time. One must always bear in mind that the Roman Empire "fell" only in the West. It endured in the East, although there, too, Greco-Roman Civilization was significantly changed. The civilization of the Eastern Empire during the medieval centuries is normally described not as "Roman" or even "Greco-Roman" but as "Byzantine,"* and the change in name betokens a profound alteration in mood. In other words, Greco-Roman culture was gradually transformed in both East and West, but its

---

*So-called because the eastern capital of Constantinople had been built on the site of the Greek colony of Byzantium.

transformation in the West was accompanied by the dismemberment of the Roman state whereas its transformation in the East occurred despite an underlying political continuity in which emperor followed emperor in more-or-less unbroken succession.

In the West, then, we are faced with two separate phenomena—political breakdown and cultural transformation. The political collapse culminated in the deposition of the last western emperor in A.D. 476, but the true period of crisis was the chaotic third century when the Empire nearly disintegrated. Viewed against the background of the third-century anarchy, the great work of reconstruction under Diocletian and Constantine seems a remarkable achievement. The strong imperial government that emerged at that time became the basis of Byzantine political organization for centuries thereafter and, indeed, made possible the millennium-long survival of the East Roman Empire. But in the West the reforms succeeded only temporarily. The death of the body politic was delayed, but the disease remained uncured.

The West had always been poorer and less urbanized than the East, and its economy, badly shaken by the political chaos of the third century, began to break down under the growing burden of imperial government and the defense of hard-pressed frontiers. Perhaps the fatal flaw in the western economy was its inability to compensate for the cessation of imperial expansion by more intensive internal development. There was no large-scale industry, no mass production; the majority of the population was far too poor to provide a mass market. Industrial production was inefficient and technology progressed at a snail's pace. The economy remained fundamentally agrarian, and farming techniques advanced little during the centuries of the Empire. The Roman plow was rudimentary; windmills were unknown and water mills exceptional. The horse could not be used as a draught animal because the Roman harness crossed the horse's windpipe and tended to strangle him when he pulled a heavy load. Consequently, Roman agriculture was based on the less efficient oxen and on the muscles of slaves and *coloni.*

Economic exhaustion brought with it the twin evils of population decline and growing poverty. At the same time that the manpower shortage was becoming acute and impoverishment was paralyzing the middle classes, the army and bureaucracy were expanding and the expenses of government were soaring. One result of these processes was the de-urbanization of the West. By the fifth century once vigorous cities were becoming ghosts of their former selves, drained of their wealth and much of their population. Only the small class of great landowners managed to prosper in the economic atmosphere of the late Western Empire, and these men now abandoned their town houses, withdrew from civic affairs, and retired to their estates where they often assembled sizable private armies and defied the tax collector. The aristocracy, having now fled the city, would remain an agrarian class for the next thousand years. The rural nobility of the Middle Ages had come into being.

The decline of the city was fatal to the urban-based administrative structure of the Western Empire. More than that, it brought an end to the urban-oriented culture of Greco-Roman antiquity. The civilization of Athens, Alexandria, and Rome could not survive in the fields. It is in the decay of urban society that we find the crucial connecting link between political collapse and cultural transformation. In a very real sense Greco-Roman culture was dead long before the final demise of the Western Empire, and the deposition of the last emperor in 476 was merely the faint postscript to a process that had been completed long before. By then the cities were dying; the rational, humanist outlook had given way to mysticism. And the desperate emperors, faced with a growing shortage of manpower and resources, were turning more and more to Germanic peoples to defend their frontiers and preserve order in their state. In the end Germans abounded in the army, entire tribes were hired to defend the frontiers, and Germanic military leaders came to hold positions of high au-

thority in the Western Empire. Survival had come to depend
on the success of half-hearted Germanic defenders against
plunder-hungry Germanic invaders.

But despite these symptoms of decay, in a certain sense
Greco-Roman culture never died in the West. It exerted a
profound influence, as we have seen, on the Doctors of the
Latin Church, and, through them, on the mind of the Middle
Ages. It was the basis of repeated cultural revivals, great and
small, down through the centuries—in the era of Charlemagne
and in the High Middle Ages, in the Italian Renaissance and
in the neo-classical eighteenth century. And if in one sense
the western half of the Roman state was dead long before its
line of emperors ended in 476, in another sense it survived
long thereafter—in the ecclesiastical organization of the Roman Catholic Church and in the medieval Holy Roman Empire. Roman law endured to inspire Western jurisprudence;
the Latin tongue remained the language of educated Euro-
peans for more than a millennium, while evolving in the
lower levels of society into the Romance languages: Italian,
French, Spanish, Portugese, and Romanian. In countless
forms the rich legacy of classical antiquity was passed on. Eu-
ropeans for centuries to come would be nourished by Greek
thought and haunted by the memory of Rome.

**The Germanic Invasions** | The German peoples had long been
a threat to the Empire. They had defeated a Roman army in
the reign of Augustus; they had probed deeply into the Empire under Marcus Aurelius and again in the mid-third century. But until the later fourth century the Romans had always managed eventually to drive the invaders out or settle
them under Roman rule. Beginning in the 370's, however, an
exhausted Empire was confronted by renewed Germanic
pressures of an unprecedented magnitude.

Lured by the relative wealth, the good soil, and the sunny
climate of the Mediterranean world, the invaders tended to
regard the Empire not as something to destroy but as something to enjoy. Their age-long yearning for the fair lands

across the Roman frontier was suddenly transformed into an urgent need by the westward thrust of a tribe of Asian nomads known as Huns. These fierce horsemen conquered one Germanic tribe after another and turned them into satellites. In about 370 the Ostrogoths fell under Hunnish domination, and the neighboring Visigoths, a kindred Germanic tribe, sought to avoid a similar disaster by requesting sanctuary behind the Empire's Danube frontier. The Eastern Emperor Valens, a fervent Arian, sympathized with the Visigoths because they were themselves converts to Arian Christianity. In 376 he permitted them to cross peacefully into the Empire.

There was trouble almost immediately. Corrupt imperial officials cheated and abused the Visigoths, who retaliated by going on a rampage. When Emperor Valens himself took the field against them, his military incapacity cost him his army and his life at the battle of Adrianople in 378. Adrianople was a military debacle of the first order. Valens' successor, the able Theodosius I, managed to pacify the Visigoths, but neither he nor any of his successors were able to expel them.

When Theodosius died in 395 Roman imperial authority was divided between his two sons. As it happened, the eastern and western halves of the Empire were never again rejoined under a single ruler. A vigorous new Visigothic leader named Alaric now led his people on a second campaign of pillage and destruction that threatened Italy itself. In 406 the desperate western emperor, an incompetent named Honorius, summoned the legions guarding the Rhine frontier to block Alaric's advance, with the disastrous consequence that the Vandals and a number of other tribes swept across the unguarded Rhine into Gaul. Shortly thereafter the Roman legions abandoned distant Britain and the island was gradually overrun by Germanic war bands. In 408 the only able general in the West was executed at the command of Emperor Honorius, who had meanwhile taken refuge behind the marshes of Ravenna. The Visigoths entered Rome unopposed in 410, and Alaric permitted them to plunder the city for three days.

The sack of Rome had a devastating impact on imperial

morale, but in historical perspective it appears as a mere inci-
dent in the disintegration of the Western Empire. The Visigoths soon left the city to its feeble emperor and turned
northward into southern Gaul and Spain where they established a kingdom that endured until the Muslim conquests of
the eighth century. Meanwhile other tribes were carving out
kingdoms of their own. The Vandals swept through Gaul and
Spain and across the Straits of Gibraltar into Africa. In 430,
the very year of St. Augustine's death, they took his city of
Hippo. A new Vandal kingdom arose in North Africa, centering on ancient Carthage. Almost immediately the Vandals began taking to the sea as buccaneers, devastating Mediterranean shipping and sacking one coastal city after another. Vandal piracy shattered the age-long peace of the Mediterranean
and dealt a crippling blow to the waning commerce of the
Western Empire.

Midway through the fifth century the Huns themselves
moved against the West, led by their chieftain Attila, the
"Scourge of God." Defeated by a Roman-Visigothic army in
Gaul in 451, they returned the following year, hurling themselves toward Rome and leaving a path of devastation behind
them. The western emperor abandoned Rome to Attila's mer-
cies, but the Roman bishop, Pope Leo I, traveled northward
from the city to negotiate with the Huns on the faint chance
that they might be persuaded to turn back. Oddly enough,
Pope Leo succeeded in his mission. Perhaps because the
health of the Hunnish army was adversely affected by the
Italian climate, perhaps because the majestic Pope Leo was
able to overawe the superstitious Attila, the Huns retired
from Italy. Shortly afterward Attila died, the Hunnish empire
collapsed, and the Huns themselves vanished from history.
They were not mourned.

In its final years the Western Empire, whose jurisdiction
now scarcely extended beyond Italy, fell under the control of
hardbitten military adventurers of Germanic birth. Emperors
continued to reign for a time, but their Germanic generals
were the powers behind the throne. In 476 a general named

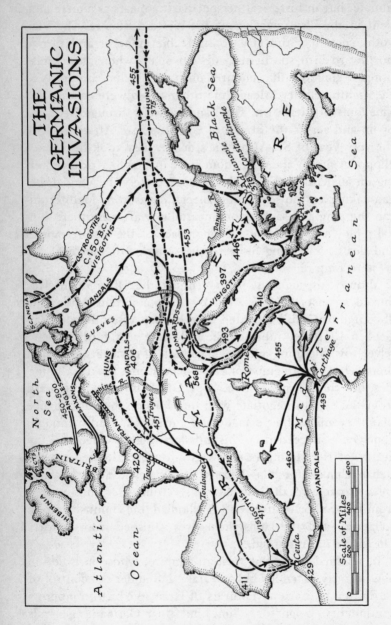

The Germanic invasions.

Odovacar, who saw no point in perpetuating the farce, de-
posed the last emperor. Sending the imperial trappings to
Constantinople, he asserted his sovereignty over Italy by confiscating a good deal of farm land for the use of his Germanic
troops. Odovacar claimed to rule as an agent of the Eastern
Empire but in fact he was on his own. A few years later the
Ostrogoths, now free of Hunnish control and led by a skillful
king named Theodoric, advanced into Italy, conquered Odovacar, and established a strong state of their own.

Theodoric ruled Italy from 493 to 526. More than any
other Germanic king he appreciated and respected Roman
culture, and in his kingdom the Arian Ostrogoths and the Orthodox Romans lived and worked together in relative harmony. Theodoric devoted much energy to repairing aque-
ducts, erecting impressive new buildings, and bringing a degree of prosperity to the long-troubled peninsula. The improved political and economic climate gave rise to a minor
intellectual revival that contributed to the transmission of
Greco-Roman culture into the Middle Ages. The philosopher
Boethius, a high official in Theodoric's regime, produced
philosophical works and translations which served as fundamental texts in western schools for the next five hundred
years. His *Consolation of Philosophy*, an interesting mixture
of Platonism and Stoicism, was immensely popular throughout the Middle Ages. Theodoric's own secretary, Cassiodorus,
was another scholar of considerable distinction. Cassiodorus
spent his later years as abbot of a monastery and set his
monks to the invaluable task of copying and preserving the
great literary works of antiquity, both Christian and pagan.

During the years of Theodoric's beneficent rule in Ostro-
gothic Italy, another famous Germanic king, Clovis (481–
511), was creating a Frankish kingdom in Gaul. Clovis was far
less Romanized, far less enlightened, far crueler than Theodoric, but his kingdom proved to be the most enduring of all
the Germanic successor states. The Franks were good farmers
as well as good soldiers, and they established deep roots in
the soil of Gaul. Moreover, the Frankish regime was buttress-

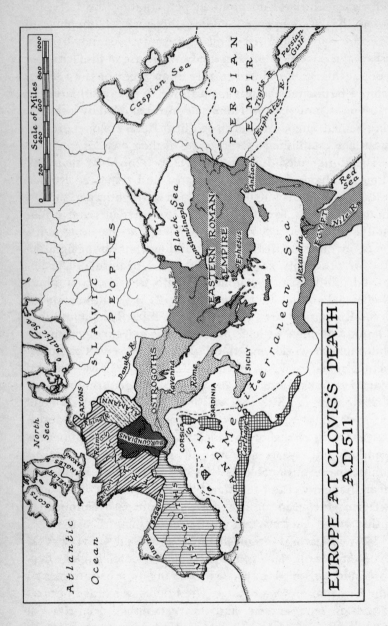

Europe at Clovis's death: A.D. 511.

ed by the enthusiastic support of the Catholic Church. For Clovis, who had been untouched by Arianism, was converted directly from Germanic paganism to Catholic Christianity. Despite his bad habit of murdering every possible political rival, Clovis came to be regarded by the Church as a God-inspired champion of Christian orthodoxy in a sea of Arianism. As the centuries went by, the royal name "Clovis" was softened to "Louis" and the "Franks" became the "French." And the friendship between the Frankish monarchy and the Church developed into one of the determining elements in European politics.

**Europe In A.D. 500** | As the sixth century dawned, the Western Empire was only a memory. In its place was a group of Germanic successor kingdoms that vaguely foreshadowed the states of modern Western Europe. Theodoric headed a tolerant and relatively enlightened Ostrogothic-Arian regime in Italy. The cruel but Orthodox Clovis was completing the Frankish conquest of Gaul. The Vandal monarchy, Arian in religion and increasingly corrupt and intolerant, lorded it over the restive population of North Africa. The Arian Visigoths were being driven out of southern Gaul by the Franks, but their regime continued to dominate Spain for the next two centuries. And in Britain various Germanic warbands— Saxons, Angles, and others—were in the process of establishing a group of small pagan kingdoms which would one day coalesce into "Angle-land" or England.

At the very time that the Germanic kingdoms were establishing themselves in the West, the Roman papacy was beginning to play an important, independent role in European society. We have seen how the mid-fifth century pope, Leo I (440–461), assumed the task of protecting the city of Rome from the Huns, winning for himself the moral leadership of the West. Leo and his successors declared that the papacy was the highest authority in the Church and, following the example of St. Ambrose, they insisted on the supremacy of Church over state in spiritual matters. In proclaiming its doctrines of papal supremacy in the Church and ecclesiastical independence from state control, the papacy was hurling a direct challenge at Byzantine caesaropapism. In the fifth century these papal doctrines remained little more than words, but they were to result in an ever-widening gulf between the Eastern and Western Church. More than that, they constitute the opening phase of the prolonged medieval struggle between the rival claims of Church and state. The mighty papacy of the High Middle Ages was yet many centuries away, but it was already foreshadowed in the bold independence of Leo I. The Western Empire was dead, but eternal Rome still claimed the allegiance of the world.

## CHRONOLOGY OF THE LATER EMPIRE

All Dates A.D.

| | |
|---|---|
| 96–180: | The age of the great second-century emperors |
| 180–192: | Reign of Commodus |
| 193–211: | Reign of Septimius Severus |
| 235–284: | Height of the anarchy; "barracks emperors" |
| 185–254: | Origen |
| 205–270: | Plotinus |
| 284–305: | Reign of Diocletian |
| 306–337: | Reign of Constantine |
| 325: | Council of Nicaea |
| 330: | Founding of Constantinople |
| 354–430: | St. Augustine of Hippo |
| 376: | Visigoths cross Danube |
| 378: | Battle of Adrianople |
| 378–395: | Reign of Theodosius I |
| 395: | Final division of Eastern and Western Empires |
| 410: | Alaric sacks Rome |
| 430: | Vandals capture Hippo |
| 451–452: | Huns invade Western Europe |
| 440–461: | Pontificate of Leo I |
| 476: | Last western emperor deposed by Odovacar |
| 493–526: | Theodoric the Ostrogoth rules Italy |
| 481–511: | Clovis rules Franks, conquers Gaul |

# PART THREE

# Suggested Readings

The asterisk indicates a paperback edition.

## General Histories of Rome

The two best single volume texts on Roman history are:

Max Cary and H. H. Scullard, *A History of Rome down to the Reign of Constantine* (3rd ed., St. Martin's Press), and A. E. R. Boak and W. G. Sinnigen, *A History of Rome to A.D. 565* (5th ed., Macmillan).

M. Rostovtzeff, *Rome* (*Oxford Galaxy). A reprint of Vol. II of Rostovtzeff's *History of the Ancient World* first published in 1927: a scholarly masterpiece which stresses social history and perhaps overestimates class antagonisms.

N. Lewis and M. Reinhold, *Roman Civilization* (*2 vols., Harper). Well-chosen selections from original sources provide a vivid picture of Rome from its origins to the triumph of Christianity.

Among the several other general accounts of Roman civilization are:

R. H. Barrow, *The Romans* (*Penguin).

Donald R. Dudley, *The Civilization of Rome* (*Mentor).

Michael Grant, *The World of Rome* (*Mentor): 133 B.C. to A.D. 217, and *The Climax of Rome* (Little, Brown), on the second and third centuries A.D.

## Republic and Early Empire

Theodor Mommsen, *The History of Rome* (*Meridian). The great classical account of the Roman Republic, written originally in the 1850's, and drastically abridged in this new edition by D. A. Saunders and J. H. Collins.

Ronald Syme, *The Roman Revolution* (*Oxford). This stimulating study stresses the political significance of the great families of the late Republic.

H. H. Scullard, *From the Gracchi to Nero* (*Praeger). A short, composite history of Roman civilization from 133 B.C. to A.D. 68.

L. R. Taylor, *Party Politics in the Age of Caesar* (*University of California Press). A detailed study of the mechanics of Roman politics, the relatives of nobles and clients, and the role of the state religion.

Samuel Dill, *Roman Society from Nero to Marcus Aurelius* (*Meridian, from the 2nd ed.). A splendid older account that still retains its value.

J. Carcopino, *Daily Life in Ancient Rome* (*Yale). An illuminating reconstruction of Roman life in the age of Trajan.

T. W. Africa, *Rome of the Caesars* (*Wiley). The first two centuries of imperial Rome are approached through the lives of eleven men ranging from Sejanus, the politician, to Galen, the doctor.

H. Mattingly, *The Man in the Roman Street* (*Norton). On everyday life.

H. Mattingly, *Roman Imperial Civilization* (*Anchor). A perceptive and significant study.

M. Yourcenar, *Memoirs of Hadrian* (*Noonday). A well-documented historical novel that reconstructs second-century Rome with extraordinary psychological depth.


## The Mystery Religions and Christianity

F. Cumont, *The Mysteries of Mithra,* translated by T. J. McCormack (*Dover), and *Oriental Religions in Roman Paganism* (*Dover). Two fundamental studies by a great scholar, outdated in details but still useful.

R. Bultmann, *Primitive Christianity in its Contemporary Setting* (*Meridian). Readable and authoritative.

R. M. Ogilvie, *The Romans and their Gods* (*Norton). For background on Roman religion in the Augustan age.

Peter Brown, *Augustine of Hippo: A Biography* (*University of California Press). An extraordinarily sensitive and perceptive recent study.

Michael Gough, *The Early Christians* (Praeger). A good popular account with fine illustrations.

E. R. Goodenough, *The Church in the Roman Empire* (*Henry Holt). A brief, lucid survey.

V. Latourette, *History of Christianity* (Harper). One of the best short histories of the Christian Church.

H. O. Taylor, *The Emergence of Christian Culture in the West* (*Harper). An ageless study by one of the masters of medieval intellectual history.

C. N. Cochrane, *Christianity and Classical Culture* (*Oxford). An interpretive tour de force, sympathetic to the rise of the mystical viewpoint.

Colm Lubheid, *The Essential Eusebius* (*Mentor). An authoritative introduction and brief commentary add depth and clarity to this translation of the writings of the first great Christian chronicler.

## The Later Empire and the Germanic Invasions

J. B. Bury, *History of the Later Roman Empire* (*2 vols., Dover). The standard account, full and authoritative, by one of the distinguished historians of this century.

F. Lot, *The End of the Ancient World and the Beginnings of the Middle Ages* (*Harper). A masterly study which places stress on the economic factors in the decline. A valuable introduction by Glanville Downey summarizes recent scholarship on the problem of "decline and fall."

Mortimer Chambers, ed., *The Fall of Rome* (*Holt, Rinehart, and Winston). Well-chosen excerpts from historical writings dealing with the decline of Rome provide a compact, illuminating survey of historical opinion on the subject.

Samuel Dill, *Roman Society in the Last Century of the Western Empire* (*Meridian). A brilliant older work.

Edward Gibbon, *The Triumph of Christendom in the Roman Empire* (*Harper). Chapters XV—XX from Gibbon's masterpiece, *The Decline and Fall of the Roman Empire*. The entire work is available in a three-volume Modern Library edition.

A. H. M. Jones, *The Later Roman Empire* (3 vols., Blackwell's). An extremely important work; a classic in the field.

Peter Brown, *The World of Late Antiquity: A.D. 150—750* (*Harcourt Brace Jovanovich). A well written, well illustrated work treating with sympathy this era of profound social and cultural change in Eastern and Western Europe and the Near East.

## Sources

B. Davenport, ed., *The Portable Roman Reader* (*Viking). One of several good anthologies now available in paperback.

There are numerous available editions of the works of Cicero, Livy, Sallust, Josephus, Petronius, Ovid, Catullus, Seneca, Marcus Aurelius, Virgil, Horace, Plutarch, Tacitus, Suetonius, and other important Roman writers many of them in paperback, which enable the student to experience Roman civilization first hand. For early Christianity the New Testament is the ideal source. Modern paperback editions of the four Gospels and the Acts of the Apostles are readily available. St. Augustine's *Confessions* has been published in several paperback editions. For the *City of God*, see Vernon J. Bourke, ed.,

*St. Augustine's City of God* (Doubleday Image). An intelligent abridgment.

Gregory of Tours, *History of the Franks,* tr. O. M. Dalton (Oxford). Provides an interesting account of Clovis and the early Franks in Gaul.

# Index

Aachen, roman emperor in, 178
Abraham, and Jews, 39-40
Academy, of Plato, 112
Achilles, 69, 110
Acropolis, 74, 91, 93, 120, 123
Actium, battle of, 168
Adrainople, battle of, 214
Aegean Sea, 37, 68, 72, 89, 90, 93
Aeneas, 171
*Aeneid* (of Virgil), 171
Aeschylus, 90
  dramas of, 120-121
Agamemnon, King of Mycenae,
  61, 67, 69
Agora, 74
Agriculture, 4-5
  and Neolithic Revolution, 4-5
Ahriman, 51
Ahura Mazda, 49
Akhnaton, Pharoah of Egypt, 32-
  34, 37, 40
Akkad, kingdom of, 15, 17, 46
Alaric, king of Visigoths, 214

Alexander the Great, 46, 51, 98,
  112, 126-129, 139, 149, 169
  and Greece, 126-129
  and Persia, 127-129
Alexandria, 128, 129, 138, 169, 189
  during Principate, 180
  Museum of, 138
  patriarch of, 188
Alphabet, 38
  Greek adoption of, 68
Ambrose, St., 205, 206, 219
  writings of, 206
Amon-Re, 26
  and Akhnaton, 32
  rivals pharaohs, 34
Amorites, 17-18
Amos, 44
Anatolia, 47
Anaximander, 104-105
Angles, 219
*Antigone* (of Sophocles), 121
Antigonids, successors to Alexander,
  131, 157

225